Knit Wild

21 sweaters with nature-inspired motifs in insulating yarns to keep you warm wherever you may roam

ANNA-SOFIA VINTERSOL

STACKPOLE BOOKS

Essex, Connecticut
Blue Ridge Summit, Pennsylvania

STACKPOLE BOOKS

An imprint of Globe Pequot, the trade division of
The Rowman & Littlefield Publishing Group, Inc.
4501 Forbes Blvd., Ste. 200
Lanham, MD 20706
www.rowman.com

Distributed by NATIONAL BOOK NETWORK
800-462-6420

Photography by Trine-Lise Løvaas and Anna-Sofia Vintersol, except as noted
Pages 34, 35, 66, 67, 100, 112, 113, 120, 121, 166, 167 by Jeanette Samira
Pages 32, 33, 36, 37 by Elisabeth Tindeland
Pages 41, 152, 153 by Erik Roberto Hetager
Pages 12, 104, 108, 109, 192, 193, 197 by Thomas Olaussen

Page 39 by Gry Sørdah
Pages 30, 225 by Crysta Haslem
Page 22 by Raven Retz
Page 28 by Lyne Ricard
Page 131 by Monica Sæterøy Høybakk
Page 29 by Marianne Pontarollo

Art and Design by Anna-Sofia Vintersol

British Library Cataloguing in Publication Information available

Library of Congress Cataloging-in-Publication Data available

ISBN 978-0-8117-7467-3 (cloth: alk. paper)
ISBN 978-0-8117-7468-0 (electronic)

First Edition

Printed in India

Contents

Preface

I've felt a special connection with the wilderness since my earliest days. While other children enjoyed playing together, I found solace and contentment playing in the woods, where I would explore, embracing the joys of muddy paths and gleeful puddle-jumping regardless of the whims of weather or season. Socializing was never my strongest suit, as I preferred indulging in arts and crafts, finding solace in the strokes of my paintbrush and the joy of creating. School was a mixed bag for me, with art being my primary interest, while subjects like history and gym managed to hold my attention. It was when I turned eleven that I received the diagnosis of Asperger's syndrome, a form of autism affectionately referred to as "the rainbow," and I've come to regard my Asperger's as the comforting hue of blue within that rainbow, my favorite color. In fact, the term "wrong planet syndrome" accurately captures how I often felt in social situations, which is why I sought refuge in the solitude of the woods, finding peace in my own company.

It was in 2018 that I discovered the art of knitting, a skill that quickly captivated my heart. With every stitch, I found myself diving deeper into the craft, allowing my creativity to flourish. Before long, I began creating my own unique designs inspired by the great outdoors, which has always been my favored sanctuary. Now, after six years of knitting, I am thrilled to share with you a carefully curated collection of my most cherished outdoor knits.

As a person of mixed German heritage, I'd also like to share a popular saying from Germany: "There is no bad weather, only bad clothing." This adage reflects the importance of being well-prepared for different weather conditions, ensuring one can truly enjoy the beauty of the outdoors. I hope this saying resonates with you as you explore the pages of this book, finding inspiration and practicality in my designs.

For more insights and to stay connected, follow me on Instagram and Facebook, where you can find me under the name @loparefur. Feel free to share your own knitted creations with me using the hashtag #AnnaSofiaVintersol.

I hope this book brings you warmth, inspiration, and a deeper appreciation for the great outdoors.

Anna-Sofia Vintersol

Yarns Perfect for Adventure

I mainly design garments for the outdoor life meant to cater to the demands of high-altitude expeditions in the snow-clad mountains of Manitoba, the rugged coastlines of the Pacific Northwest, and the wild forests of Alaska. I exclusively work with pure wool made from Icelandic, Peruvian, Norwegian, and North American sheep breeds. Wool possesses remarkable qualities that make it an excellent choice for outdoor wear. It is self-cleaning, efficiently repelling dirt and stains, allowing your garments to stay fresh even in the harshest environments. Additionally, wool's natural water-resistance provides a layer of defense against rain and dampness, keeping you dry during your outdoor pursuits.

Let me unveil a list of yarns that captivate my adventurous spirit:

Icelandic Wool from the robust Icelandic sheep, this wool boasts an unrivaled resilience, preserving your body's warmth even in the most extreme sub-zero temperatures. It is a water-repellent sheep's wool perfect for cold weather and outdoor activities. Natural colors and rustic charm add to its appeal. It is ideal for crafting traditional garments and knitwear. Icelandic wool is the ultimate outdoor wool.

North American Wool is a diverse and abundant resource, hailing from a multitude of sheep breeds thriving in the continent's vast landscapes. Rambouillet, Columbia, Targhee, Shetland, Corriedale, Border Leicester, Romney, and Lincoln are just a few examples of North American wool. From the soft and delicate fibers of certain breeds to the sturdy and unyielding strands of others, this wool encompasses a wide spectrum of possibilities. Whether you seek a cozy and gentle touch for a lightweight layer or a robust and rugged yarn for outdoor exploration, North American wool offers an array of choices, ensuring that every adventurer can find their perfect match for any journey.

Peruvian Highland Wool is a premium natural fiber known for its warmth, softness, and resilience. Sourced from sheep in the high-altitude regions of Peru, this wool is highly valued in the textile industry for producing cozy and durable clothing and accessories.

Norwegian Wool The pride of Norway's sheep breeds, this wool is an embodiment of endurance and fortitude. Its natural lanolin-laden fibers enhance water resistance and shield you from the relentless assault of rain and wind while keeping you stylishly snug.

Merino Wool is known for its exceptional softness. It has excellent moisture-wicking properties, meaning it can absorb and release moisture to keep the wearer dry and comfortable. Merino wool is also renowned for its insulating capabilities, providing warmth in cold weather and staying breathable in warmer conditions. Due to its natural properties, Merino wool is well-suited for outdoor activities. It can regulate body temperature, making it comfortable to wear in various weather conditions. Additionally, it resists odors and is hypoallergenic, making it an ideal choice for those with sensitive skin.

As you enter your adventure, remember that the choice of materials can make or break your experience. With the resolute might of wool by your side, you can confidently face the elements, for my designs are crafted to withstand the test of time and enable you to conquer uncharted lands with these warm and durable comrades.

Soft and Cozy Yarn Alternatives

Outdoor wools may not be the most comfortable option for everyone due to their somewhat "scratchy" nature. If you happen to have a sensitivity, you might find Merino wool to be a preferred choice, known for its exceptional softness, durability, and inherent weather resistance. Merino fibers possess natural elasticity, making them comfortable to wear while providing ample insulation and moisture-wicking properties. In other words: Merino is perfect for outdoor garments. Additionally, it resists odors and is hypoallergenic, making it an ideal choice for those with sensitive skin.

While alpaca yarn offers luxurious softness, it may not be the most suitable choice for outdoor use due to its tendency to absorb moisture. Alpaca fibers have excellent thermal properties, but their absorption capability can lead to dampness in wet conditions, therefore I recommend alpaca yarn only for indoor garments.

If pure wool is not your fiber of choice or if you are allergic to wool, cotton yarn is a fantastic option for warm weather, and it doesn't have the scratchiness associated with some wool fibers. It's also easy to care for and can withstand the elements reasonably well. Just keep in mind that cotton doesn't provide the same insulation as wool, so it is not suitable for extremely cold conditions.

Another alternative is acrylic yarn, which is a synthetic option that is often chosen for outdoor wear due to its durability and resistance to moisture. It's also less likely to stretch or shrink when exposed to the elements. Acrylic yarn comes in a wide variety of colors and can mimic the appearance of wool, making it a versatile choice for different outdoor projects. However, it will not provide the same natural warmth as wool.

Alternatives for Gauge 13–14 stitches = 4 in (10 cm) on US 10 (6 mm) needle in stockinette stitch

Brands like Malabrigo, Woolfolk, and Blue Sky Fibers offer Merino wool yarns in Bulky or Chunky weights that can serve as excellent substitutes. These yarns provide the cozy comfort and exceptional stitch definition that you desire and are super soft.

Alternatives for Gauge 18–19 stitches = 4 in (10 cm) on US 10 (6 mm) needle in stockinette stitch

For a similar gauge and comparable qualities consider Merino wool yarns in a DK (double knitting) or worsted weight category. Brands like Malabrigo, Madelinetosh, and Brooklyn Tweed offer Merino wool yarns in DK and worsted weights, which can serve as wonderful substitutes. These yarns deliver exceptional stitch definition, warmth, and a soft hand feel, making them suitable for a wide range of projects.

Alternatives for Gauge 20–23 stitches = 4 in (10 cm) on US 6 (4 mm) needle in stockinette stitch

For a similar gauge range, look for Merino wool yarns in the fingering or sport weight categories. These weights typically align well with the specified gauge and provide a delicate yet substantial fabric. Brands such as Malabrigo, Hedgehog Fibres, and Cascade Yarns offer Merino wool yarns in fingering and sport weights that are perfect substitutes.

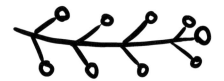

Gauge measurements should always be taken after blocking.

Yarns Used in this Book

Here is a list of the commonly used yarns in the patterns in this book.

Ístex Léttlopi is probably the most famous Icelandic yarn that has captured the hearts of knitting enthusiasts worldwide. Ístex Léttlopi is loosely spun, giving it a unique texture and adding a touch of character to your knitting projects. Its loose structure also enhances its insulating properties, providing a warm and cozy feel ideal for cooler climates.

Ístex Álafosslopi is Istex Léttlopi's older cousin—the ultimate yarn for cold climates! It is a bulky, thick yarn perfect for creating warm sweaters that defy winter's chill. Crafters and knitters worldwide appreciate Álafosslopi for its ability to withstand harsh conditions while keeping you comfortably warm. The colors are natural and, from the rugged volcanic terrains to the vibrant hues of the Northern Lights, this yarn captures the essence of Iceland's natural beauty.

Ístex Plötulopi is made from pure unspun Icelandic wool. Sweaters knitted with this yarn are lighter and airier than Léttlopi. Knitting with just one strand can be complicated, as unspun yarn breaks easily. Therefore, it is often a good idea to combine it with other yarns, such as lace and strands of mohair. This two-strand combination will be easier to work with and makes the overall garment softer.

Brooklyn Tweed Tones is known for its rich, intense colors which are unmatched, and its exceptional stitch definition brings colorwork to life. Sweaters knitted in this yarn are vibrant, durable, and showcase impeccable stitch work.
Brooklyn Tweed Tones can be used interchangeably with:

Brooklyn Tweed Shelter. Rustic charm meets versatile style. Made from 100% American wool, this yarn combines warmth and durability with a modern twist. Its unique woolen-spun construction delivers a lofty texture and excellent stitch definition. With a wide array of subtly heathered colors and with its high-quality fibers and impressive performance, it offers an extensive palette that adds depth and richness to every garment.

Brooklyn Tweed Quarry. Chunky, cozy, and captivating, this yarn is expertly crafted from 100% American Targhee-Columbia wool, ensuring exceptional texture and warmth for any project. Its lofty three-ply structure enhances stitch definition, creating stunning patterns with a touch of luxury. Thanks to its superb warmth-to-weight ratio, this yarn is ideal for thicker garments that offer both coziness and comfort. For added versatility, I love pairing it with two strands of Brooklyn Tweed Shelter or Tones, resulting in beautifully defined stitches and a garment that is both warm and lightweight.

Kelbourne Woolens Scout is a strong, versatile, heathered 100% wool yarn. The wool in Scout is a cross between Corriedale and Merino. It is not as soft as Merino, but it is stronger and more durable. Scout is also unique in that it is a heather, meaning multiple colors are pre-blended prior to spinning to create a shade with a lot of depth and variation. Natural is the one exception to this—it is the undyed white shade of wool.

Kelbourne Woolens Germantown is a quick-knitting 100% USA-made non-superwash worsted wool known for its softness, bounce, and stitch definition.

Kelbourne Woolens Lucky Tweed is a 100% Merino wool yarn and authentic Donegal Tweed yarn made in Donegal, Ireland. It features colorful tweed neps blended with wool fibers, creating a charming speckled effect throughout the yarn. It is known for its warmth and durability.

Malabrigo Chunky is a super-soft and bulky yarn crafted from 100% Merino wool. With its thick and plush texture, this yarn is perfect for quick and cozy projects. Its vibrant and richly dyed colors provide both warmth and style in one delightful package.

Malabrigo Worsted is a 100% Merino wool yarn hand-dyed in stunning colors, showcasing beautiful tonal variations. Its soft and squishy texture adds a cozy feel to any sweater.

Malabrigo Rios is a 100% superwash Merino wool yarn. Soft, strong, and washable, this 4-ply gem resists pilling and suits well-loved garments. This stunning yarn is a workhorse! The plies help resist pilling, and washability makes it fantastic for frequently-worn garments. It comes in an array of watercolor-multi, semi-solid, and variegated colorways.

Spincycle Plump is a bulky-weight yarn known for its stunning color transitions and rich texture. Hand-dyed and handspun in the USA, it creates mesmerizing marled effects. Every skein is like a snowflake, a fingerprint, a seashell, or the wing of a dragonfly—one-of-a-kind, like every knitted project. Versatile and visually striking, it's perfect for adding artistry to your sweaters.

Rauma Vams is made from 100% Norwegian pure new wool, which gives it a soft and natural feel. Due to its natural wool composition, Rauma Vams yarn provides warmth and insulation, making it ideal for creating cozy and comfortable pieces. It is also known for its durability, ensuring that the finished projects will stand the test of time.

Rosa Pomar Beiroa is a 100% Portuguese wool yarn known for its rustic texture and earthy colors. It's great for outdoor knitwear due to its warmth and sustainability, sourced from ethical farming practices.

Tips

Great tips for beginners or a refresher for veterans

Check Your Gauge

It's a good idea to check your gauge, especially if you're new to knitting or working with a new yarn. Yarns with different fiber content or thickness can yield different results, so adjusting your needle size accordingly is key to maintaining the pattern's desired measurements.

Testing your gauge ensures that your finished project will match the pattern's intended measurements.

To check your gauge, simply knit a swatch using the recommended needle size. If your stitches appear too tight and don't match the specified gauge, consider switching to a larger needle size. Conversely, if your stitches appear too loose, try using a smaller needle size. This simple adjustment helps you achieve the desired tension and ensures your project turns out just right.

How to Choose the Right Size

When selecting a size for your project, prioritize the stated measurements for the chest in the pattern. The pattern specifies the garment's finished measurements after blocking. Remember, the length of the garment can always be adjusted to suit your preferences. Keep in mind that some garments are designed to have a tighter fit, while others offer a looser silhouette.

To determine the ideal size for you, carefully examine the chest measurements provided in the pattern. Consider the fit you desire and compare these measurements to a sweater you already own which you believe has the desired dimensions. This comparison will help guide you in choosing the size that aligns with your preferred fit.

Yarn Alternatives

When considering yarn alternatives, it's important to pay attention to the yarn length and recommended needle sizes indicated on the yarn label. Yarn length plays a significant role in determining how many skeins will be required for your project when using an alternative yarn. By checking the yarn length and recommended needle sizes, you can make an informed decision about which alternative yarn is suitable for the pattern. This ensures that you have the correct amount of yarn needed to achieve the desired outcome.

Color Combinations

If you're looking for color inspiration for your project, my Instagram profile @loparefur is a great place to start. Explore the #annasofiavintersol or #knitwild hashtags to discover a vibrant community of knitters showcasing their beautiful color combinations. From subtle hues to bold palettes, you'll find a range of ideas to spark your creativity.

Steeking or working back and forth

When faced with the choice between steeking and working back and forth in a sweater pattern, each option presents unique advantages.

Steeking offers a seamless aesthetic with faster knitting and minimal purling, yet it may be perceived as daunting due to the additional finishing steps involved. On the other hand, opting for working back and forth simplifies the construction process, eliminating the need for steeking. However, this choice may result in visible seams, a slightly slower knitting pace, and a greater amount of purling. Ultimately, the decision hinges on individual preferences and comfort levels in navigating these techniques.

Guide to Blocking

To achieve optimal results, it's important to wash your garment once it has been knitted. Begin by gently hand-washing the garment in lukewarm water using a mild wool detergent. Allow the garment to soak for approximately 10 minutes, taking care not to rub or twist it. Give it a final rinse and, for a softer surface, consider adding a small amount of rinse aid, hair conditioner (without silicone), or apple cider vinegar to the last rinse water.

Wrap the garment in a towel and gently remove any remaining water by standing on the towel. Instead of laying the garment flat on a towel, which can lead to potential mold, opt for laying it on a plastic bag or a mesh drying rack. This allows for proper air circulation and drying. Gently shape the garment to its desired form, ensuring it is not stretched or distorted, and allow it to dry completely.

Converting a Pattern

When you come across a yarn that you absolutely adore, but the gauge doesn't quite match the pattern by 1 stitch per 4 in (10 cm), there's a simple solution. If the pattern specifies a gauge of 14 stitches, but your chosen yarn yields a gauge of 13 stitches, consider knitting one size smaller. Conversely, if the gauge would give you 15 stitches per 4 in (10 cm), knit one size larger.

By adjusting the size based on the gauge, you can ensure that your finished project maintains the intended measurements and proportions. This simple modification allows you to use the yarn you love while still achieving the desired fit.

The beauty of knitting lies in its versatility, which allows customization and personalization

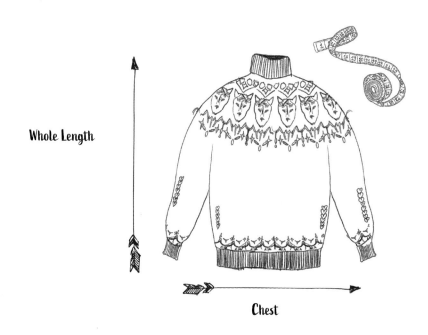

Whole Length

Chest

The Art of Colorwork

Colorwork can be intimidating, but with just a little bit of practice you can become adept at it quickly. Here are a few tips which helped me to master the art of colorwork.

Color Dominance

To achieve clean colorwork in your knitting, it's essential to pay attention to color dominance and maintain consistency.

Keep the same color in the same position throughout your work. The dominant color should be held in your left hand, while the background color is held in your right hand.

For improved tension and neater floats, I suggest catching the floats of the non-working color when knitting three to five stitches in a different color. This technique helps to secure the floats and prevent them from becoming too loose or visible on the right side of your project.

Tension

When working colorwork, achieving the right tension is key to a successful outcome. If your colorwork appears tight and creates a fabric with a higher gauge, it may be beneficial to go up a needle size. This adjustment helps to accommodate the additional thickness and texture created by multiple strands of yarn, resulting in more balanced and visually appealing colorwork.

In situations where tension remains an issue, an alternative approach is to turn your work completely inside out and knit with the inside facing outward. This method can help alleviate tension by providing a looser and more forgiving gauge.

Color Contrast

Here's a magical tip for achieving the perfect color contrast in your sweater:

If you're uncertain whether the colors you've chosen offer enough distinction, try this simple trick. Take a photo of all the yarn skeins together and either print it as a black-and-white image or apply a black and white filter to the photo. By examining the grayscale tones, you can determine if the colors provide sufficient contrast. If the shades of gray showcase a noticeable difference, then you've found a winning combination!

Coldfoot
&
Wiseman

Inspired by two small towns nestled in the Alaskan wilderness: Coldfoot and Wiseman. Once a home for gold prospectors and adventurers, these towns now have populations smaller than a family of snow owls. Yet, their simplicity and charm make them intriguing. With this in mind I wanted to design a sweater which is classic but yet sweet and cozy just like a warm hug from a fluffy snow fox. This sweater will ensure you stay warm and won't get any "cold feet," even in the coldest of snowstorms.

Coldfoot & Wiseman

This pattern is worked seamlessly in the round from the bottom up. First, the body and sleeves are worked up separately. Then, the body and sleeves are joined to form the yoke, which is worked in the round on a circular needle and shaped with decreases. The sweater is finished with a folded neck.

Sizes
(2XS, XS, S) (M, L, XL) (2XL, 3XL, 4XL)

Recommended ease: 4 in (10 cm) positive ease

Measurements
Chest circumference:
(31.5, 33.5, 36.6) (40.2, 43.3, 46.5) (50.0, 53.2, 56.7) in/
(80, 85, 93) (102, 110, 118) (127, 135, 144) cm

Arm circumference:
(11.4, 13.0, 13.0) (13.4, 13.4, 15.0) (15.0, 16.9, 17.7) in/
(29, 33,33) (34, 34, 38) (38, 43, 45) cm

Yarn
Rosa Pomar Beiroa; DK/light worsted weight;
100% Portuguese wool; 251 yd (230 m), 3.5 oz (100 g) per skein

C1: 685 Anthracite: (3, 4, 4) (4, 4, 5) (5, 5, 6) skeins
C2: 573 Mustard: (1, 1, 1) (1, 1, 1) (1, 1, 1) skein
C3: 570 Persimmon: (1, 1, 1) (1, 2, 2) (2, 2, 2) skeins
C4: 536 Tea Rose: (1, 1, 1) (1, 1, 1) (1, 1, 1) skein
C5: 401 Undyed White: (1, 1, 1) (1, 1, 1) (1, 1, 1) skein
C6: 688 Sea: (1, 1, 1) (1, 1, 1) (1, 2, 2) skeins

Needles
Double-pointed needles: US 4 and US 6 (3.5 mm and 4.5 mm)
(unless the magic loop technique is used)
Circular needles, 16 in (40 cm): US 4 and US 6 (3.5 mm and 4 mm)
Circular needles, 32 in (80 cm): US 4 and US 6 (3.5 mm and 4 mm)

Gauge
19 stitches and 26 rows = 4 in (10 cm) on US 6 needle in
stockinette stitch

Body

Cast on (152, 160, 176) (192, 208, 224) (240, 256, 272) stitches with C1 using size US 4 (3.5 mm) circular needle. Place a stitch marker to mark the beginning of the round and after (76, 80, 88) (96, 104, 112) (120, 128, 136) stitches to mark the front and back pieces.

Work "knit 1, purl 1" rib for 3 in (7.5 cm).

Change to a US 6 (4 mm) circular needle. Continue in stockinette stitch until work measures (12.6, 12.6, 12.6) (13.4, 14.2, 15.0) (15.0, 15.0, 15.7) in/(32, 32, 32) (34, 36, 38) (38, 38, 40) cm or desired length, allowing 4.7 in (12 cm) for Chart B.

Work Chart B.

Place the first (7, 9, 8) (8, 11, 11) (14, 18, 18) stitches of the round on a holder or waste yarn. The stitches for the other armhole will be put on holder when you start the yoke. Set the work aside and begin sleeves.

Sleeves

Cast on (36, 36, 36) (36, 42, 42) (42, 48, 48) stitches with C2 using size US 4 (3.5 mm) circular needle. Place a stitch marker to mark the beginning of the round.

Work "knit 1, purl 1" rib for 3 in (7.5 cm).

Change to size US 6 (4 mm) circular needle. Knit 1 round in C1.

Work pattern according to Chart A. Continue in stockinette stitch increasing 2 stitches every 5th round (1 stitch after the first stitch of the round, and 1 stitch before the last st of the round) until you have (56, 64, 64) (64, 72, 72) (80, 88, 90) stitches.

Continue in stockinette stitch until work measures (14.2, 14.2, 14.6) (15.0, 15.4, 15.7) (15.7, 16.1, 16.1) in/(36, 36, 37) (38, 39, 40) (40, 41, 41) cm or desired length, allowing 4.7 in (12 cm) for Chart B.

Work Chart B.

Place the first (8, 9, 9) (8, 12, 11) (15, 18, 19) stitches of the round on a stitch holder or waste yarn. Knit the second sleeve like the first.

Yoke

Join body and sleeves on a US 6 (4 mm) circular needle. Place a stitch marker to mark the beginning of the round at the first join. Knit over first sleeve. Work the front piece. Transfer next (7, 9, 8) (8, 11, 11) (14, 18, 18) stitches onto a stitch holder or waste yarn for underarm. Knit over the other sleeve and back piece. You should now have (234, 252, 270) (288, 306, 324) (342, 360, 378) stitches.

Work pattern according to Chart C and decrease as directed. Change to shorter needle when necessary. After completing chart (78, 84, 90) (96, 102, 108) (114, 120, 126) stitches remain on needles.

Neck

Change to size US 4 (3.5 mm) needle. Knit 1 round with C2, decreasing (0, 0, 2), (6, 10, 12), (14, 16, 18) stitches evenly over the round. You should now have (78, 84, 88) (90, 92, 96) (100, 104, 108) stitches on needles.

Work "knit 1, purl 1" rib for 3.2 in (8 cm). Bind off loosely.

Finishing

Graft the underarm stitches to close, then weave in all ends. Block the garment and lay it flat to dry. Finally, fold neck and sew in.

Coldfoot & Wiseman
ROSA POMAR Beiroa
C1: 400 Undyed Brown
C2: 675 Cinza
C3: 401 Undyed White
C4: 409 Bege
C5: 724 Cobalto
C6: 625 Verde Tropa

Coldfoot & Wiseman
BROOKLYN TWEED Shelter and Tones, THE
FARMER'S DAUGHTER FIBERS Oh Dang! held
together with Pishkun
C1: Oh Dang! Salmon Berry + Pishkun Hacer
C2: Oh Dang! I've Got Dreams to Remember +
Pishkun Union Street State of Mind
C3: Shelter Old World
C4: Tones Persimmon
C5: Shelter Bale
C6: Oh Dang! Juniper + Hand Dyed Pishkun

Chart A

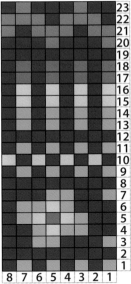

- ■ Color 1
- ■ Color 2
- □ Color 3
- ■ Color 4
- ■ Color 5
- ■ Color 6
- ⟍ Decrease left leaning
- ⟋ Decrease right leaning

Chart B

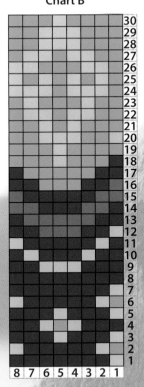

Chart C

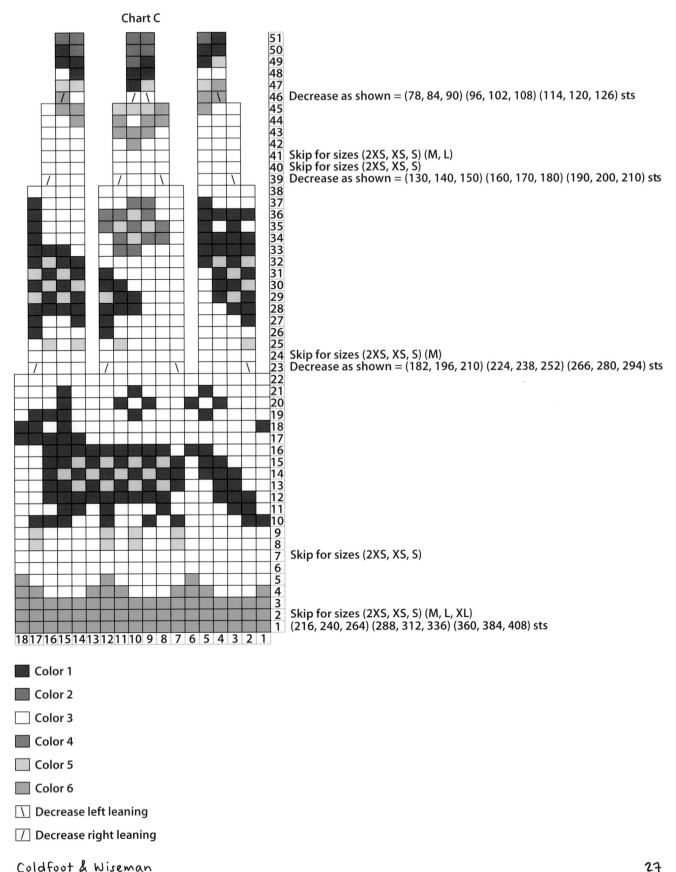

51
50
49
48
47
46 Decrease as shown = (78, 84, 90) (96, 102, 108) (114, 120, 126) sts
45
44
43
42
41 Skip for sizes (2XS, XS, S) (M, L)
40 Skip for sizes (2XS, XS, S)
39 Decrease as shown = (130, 140, 150) (160, 170, 180) (190, 200, 210) sts
38
37
36
35
34
33
32
31
30
29
28
27
26
25
24 Skip for sizes (2XS, XS, S) (M)
23 Decrease as shown = (182, 196, 210) (224, 238, 252) (266, 280, 294) sts
22
21
20
19
18
17
16
15
14
13
12
11
10
9
8
7 Skip for sizes (2XS, XS, S)
6
5
4
3
2 Skip for sizes (2XS, XS, S) (M, L, XL)
1 (216, 240, 264) (288, 312, 336) (360, 384, 408) sts

18 17 16 15 14 13 12 11 10 9 8 7 6 5 4 3 2 1

■ Color 1

■ Color 2

☐ Color 3

■ Color 4

☐ Color 5

■ Color 6

⟍ Decrease left leaning

⟋ Decrease right leaning

Coldfoot & Wiseman
SONDER YARN CO. Sunday Morning
DK
C1: Hydrate
C2: Copper Kettle
C3: Toast & Honey
C4: Flat White
C5: Cut Flowers
C6: Dreamstate

Coldfoot & Wiseman
WOOLDREAMERS Mota
C1: Mota Hand Dyed
C2: Mota 800 Beige
C3: Mota 150G Rust
C4: Mota 840 Mustard
C5: Mota 718G Turquoise
C6: Mota 912 Khaki

Coldfoot & Wiseman
KNIT PICKS Wool of the Andes Worsted
C1: Larch Heather
C2: Spruce
C3: Chestnut
C4: Garnet Heather
C5: Cilanto Heather
C6: Hand Dyed

Coldfoot & Wiseman
BROOKLYN TWEED Shelter and Tones, THE
FARMER'S DAUGHTER Oh Dang! held together
with Pishkun
C1: Oh Dang! Salmon Berry + Pishkun Hacer
C2: Oh Dang! I've Got Dreams to Remember +
Pishkun Union Street State of Mind
C3: Shelter Old World
C4: Tones Persimmon
C5: Shelter Bale
C6: Oh Dang! Juniper + Hand Dyed Pishkun

Warg Polaris

Warg Polaris is my most popular pattern, knitted and worn
by knitters around the globe. This design holds a special
place in the hearts of dog owners and mushers alike. Drawing
inspiration from the wolf, the majestic ancestor of our
faithful canine companions, Warg Polaris celebrates the deep
connection between humans and these remarkable creatures.

Warg Polaris

This pattern is worked seamlessly in the round from the bottom up. First, the body and sleeves are worked up separately. Then, the body and arms are joined to form the yoke, which is worked in the round on a circular needle and shaped with decreases. The sweater is finished with a turtleneck.

Sizes
(2XS, XS, S) (M, L, XL) (2XL, 3XL, 4XL)

Recommended ease: 4 in (10 cm) positive ease

Measurements
Chest circumference:
(31.6, 36.3, 38.7) (43.8, 46.2, 49.8) (53.3, 56, 58.5) in/
(80, 92, 98) (111, 117, 126) (135, 142, 148) cm

Arm circumference:
(14.6, 15, 16.2) (16.8, 18.2, 19) (19.7, 20.5, 21.7) in/
(37, 38, 41) (43, 46, 48) (50, 52, 55) cm

Yarn
Ístex Álafosslopi; bulky weight; 100% new Icelandic wool; 109 yd
(99.5 m), 3.5 oz (100 g) per skein

C1: 0057 Grey: (4, 4, 5) (5, 5, 6) (6, 7, 7) skeins
C2: 0054 Ash: (2, 2, 2) (2, 2, 2) (3, 3, 3) skeins
C3: 0085 Oatmeal: (2, 2, 2) (2, 2, 2) (2, 2, 2) skeins
C4: 0052 Black Sheep: (1, 1, 1) (1, 1, 1) (1, 1, 1) skeins

Needles
Double-pointed needles: US 7 and US 10 (4.5 mm and 6 mm) (unless the magic loop technique is used)
Circular needles, 16 in (40 cm): US 7 and US 10 (4.5 mm and 6 mm)
Circular needles, 32 in (80 cm): US 7 and US 10 (4.5 mm and 6 mm)

Gauge
13 stitches and 18 rows = 4 in (10 cm) on US 10 (6 mm) needle in stockinette stitch

Body
Cast on (100, 120, 126) (144, 148, 160) (172, 180, 192) stitches with C2 using size US 7 (4.5 mm) needle. Place a stitch marker to mark the beginning of the round.
Work "knit 2, purl 2" for 3 in (7.5 cm).
Change to size US 10 (6 mm) needle. Knit 1 round. Work Chart A.
Knit 1 round with C1, increase (2, 0, 2) (0, 2, 2) (2, 4, 0) stitches evenly over the round. You should now have (104, 120, 128) (144, 152, 164) (176, 184, 192) stitches on needles. Place a second marker after (52, 60, 64) (72, 76, 82) (88, 92, 96) stitches to mark front and back sides.
Continue in stockinette stitch with C1 until work measures (16.6, 16.6, 16.6) (17.4, 18.2, 19) (19, 19, 19.8) in/(42, 42, 42) (44, 46, 48) (48, 48, 50) cm or desired length.
Place the first (5, 6, 6) (6, 6, 6) (7, 6, 6) and the last (5, 5, 5) (6, 6, 6) (6, 6, 6) stitches on a stitch holder or waste yarn for underarm, a total of (10, 11, 11) (12, 12, 12) (13, 12, 12) stitches. The stitches for the other armhole will be put on holder when you start the Yoke. Set the work aside and begin sleeves.

Sleeves
Cast on (36, 36, 36) (36, 36, 40) (40, 40, 40) stitches with C2 using size US 7 (4.5 mm) needles. Place a stitch marker to mark the beginning of the round.
Work "knit 2 purl 2" rib for 3 in (7.5 cm).
Change to size US 10 (6 mm) needles. Knit 1 round with C2, increasing (0, 0, 0) (0, 0, 2) (2, 2, 2) stitches evenly over the round. You should now have (36, 36, 36) (36, 36, 42) (42, 42, 42) stitches on needles.
Work Chart A.
Continue in stockinette stitch with C1 increasing 2 stitches every 5th round (1 stitch after the first stitch of the round, and 1 stitch before the last stitch of the round) until you have (48, 50, 54) (56, 60, 62) (66, 68, 72) stitches.
Continue in stockinette stitch until work measures (17.8, 18.2, 18.2) (19, 20.1, 20.5) (20.5, 20.5, 22.1) in/(45, 46, 46) (48, 51, 52) (52, 52, 56) cm or desired length.

Place the first (5, 6, 6) (6, 6, 6) (7, 6, 6) and the last (5, 5, 5) (6, 6, 6) (6, 6, 6) stitches onto a holder or waste yarn for underarm, a total of (10, 11, 11) (12, 12, 12) (13, 12, 12) stitches.
Knit the second sleeve like the first.

Yoke
Join body and sleeves on size US 10 (6 mm) circular needle. Place a stitch marker to mark the beginning of the round at the first join. Knit over first sleeve. Knit over front side. Transfer next (10, 11, 11) (12, 12, 12) (13, 12, 12) stitches onto a holder or waste yarn for underarm. Knit over the other sleeve and back side. You should now have (160, 176, 192) (208, 224, 240) (256, 272, 288) stitches.
Work pattern according to Chart B and decrease as directed. Change to shorter needle if necessary. After completing chart (60, 66, 72) (78, 84, 90) (96, 102, 108) stitches remain on needles.

Neck
Change to size US 7 (4.5 mm) needle.
Knit 1 round with C2, decreasing (0, 2, 4) (2, 4, 6) (12, 18, 20) stitches evenly over the round. You should now have (60, 64, 68) (76, 80, 84) (84, 84, 88) stitches on needles.
Work "knit 2, purl 2" rib for 8 in (20 cm). Bind off loosely.

Finishing
Graft the underarm stitches to close, then weave in all ends. Block the garment and lay it flat to dry. Finally, fold the neck.

Warg Polaris
ÍSTEX Álafosslopi
C1: 1230 Highland Green
(C1 Wolf: 0053 Acorn)
C2: 0054 Ash
C3: 0085 Oatmeal
C4: 0052 Black Sheep

Chart B

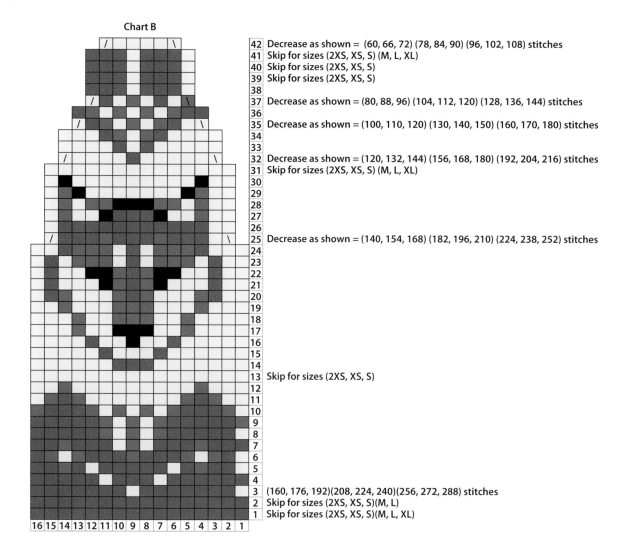

Row	Instruction
42	Decrease as shown = (60, 66, 72) (78, 84, 90) (96, 102, 108) stitches
41	Skip for sizes (2XS, XS, S) (M, L, XL)
40	Skip for sizes (2XS, XS, S)
39	Skip for sizes (2XS, XS, S)
38	
37	Decrease as shown = (80, 88, 96) (104, 112, 120) (128, 136, 144) stitches
36	
35	Decrease as shown = (100, 110, 120) (130, 140, 150) (160, 170, 180) stitches
34	
33	
32	Decrease as shown = (120, 132, 144) (156, 168, 180) (192, 204, 216) stitches
31	Skip for sizes (2XS, XS, S) (M, L, XL)
30	
29	
28	
27	
26	
25	Decrease as shown = (140, 154, 168) (182, 196, 210) (224, 238, 252) stitches
24	
23	
22	
21	
20	
19	
18	
17	
16	
15	
14	
13	Skip for sizes (2XS, XS, S)
12	
11	
10	
9	
8	
7	
6	
5	
4	
3	(160, 176, 192)(208, 224, 240)(256, 272, 288) stitches
2	Skip for sizes (2XS, XS, S)(M, L)
1	Skip for sizes (2XS, XS, S)(M, L, XL)

16 15 14 13 12 11 10 9 8 7 6 5 4 3 2 1

Chart A

10 9 8 7 6 5 4 3 2 1

6 5 4 3 2 1

- ■ Color 1
- □ Color 2
- ■ Color 3
- ■ Color 4
- \ Decrease left leaning
- / Decrease right leaning

38

Knit Wild

Warg Polaris
RAUMA Vams
C1: 03 Light Grey
C2: 13 Grey
C3: 307 Myr
C4: 36 Black

Warg Polaris
ÍSTEX Álafosslopi plus BROOKLYN
TWEED shelter held together with
RAUMA Finull
C1: Shelter Bale + Finull 4076 Golden
C2: 0054 Ash
C3: 0085 Oatmeal
C4: 0053 Acorn

Biboon
ÍSTEX Léttlopi
C1: 0051 White
C2: 9419 Ocean Blue
C3: 9434 Crimson Red
C4: 1407 Pine Green
C5: 1704 Apricot
C6: 9427 Rust
C7: 0086 Light Beige
C8: 0085 Oatmeal

Biboon

Rooted in my family's ties to the Anishinaabe, this design draws
inspiration from a dear friend who carries the legacy of her tribe as
a spokesperson. The Winter Maker, known as Biboon, is the bringer
of winter. This sweater is a tribute to the rich cultural heritage and a
celebration of the enduring spirit of the Anishinaabe people.

Biboon
- The Wintermaker

Starting with a ribbed hem, the body and sleeves are worked bottom up in the round and knit separately. A steek is added to the body for later arm attachment. The neck is knitted by picking up stitches from the body. The arms are knitted separately and sewn into the body afterwards.

Sizes
(2XS, XS, S) (M, L, XL) (2XL, 3XL, 4XL)

Recommended ease: 4 in (10 cm) positive ease

Measurements
Chest circumference:
(32.7, 35, 37) (39.4, 43.7, 48) (52.4, 56.7, 61) in/
(83, 89, 94) (100, 111, 122) (133, 144, 155) cm
Arm circumference:
(23.6, 23.6, 28.4) (28.4, 28.4, 33.1) (33.1, 37.8, 42.5) in/
(60, 60, 72) (72, 72, 84) (84, 96, 108) cm

Yarn
Ístex Léttlopi; worsted weight; 100% new Icelandic wool;
109 yd (99.5 m), 1.8 oz (50 g) per skein

C1: 0051 White: (3, 3, 3) (4, 4, 4) (5, 5, 5) skeins
C2: 1418 Straw: (2, 2, 2) (2, 2, 2) (3, 3, 3) skeins
C3: 1419 Barley: (2, 2, 2) (2, 2, 2) (3, 3, 3) skeins
C4: 9434 Crimson Red: (2, 2, 2) (2, 2, 2) (3, 3, 3) skeins
C5: 9431 Brick: (2, 2, 2) (2, 2, 2) (3, 3, 3) skeins
C6: 1412 Pink: (2, 2, 2) (2, 2, 2) (3, 3, 3) skeins
C7: 9419 Ocean Blue: (1, 1, 2) (2, 2, 2) (2, 3, 3) skeins
C8: 9420 Navy Blue: (1, 1, 2) (2, 2, 2) (2, 3, 3) skeins

Needles
Double-pointed needles: US 4 and US 7 (3.5 mm and 4.5 mm) (unless the magic loop technique is used)
Circular needles, 16 in (40 cm): US 4 and US 7 (3.5 mm and 4.5 mm)
Circular needles, 32 in (80 cm): US 4 and US 7 (3.5 mm and 4.5 mm)

Gauge
18 stitches and 26 rows = 4 in (10 cm) on US 7 needle in stockinette stitch

Body

Cast on (148, 160, 168) (180, 200, 220) (240, 260, 280) stitches with C1 using size US 4 (3.5 mm) needle. Place a stitch marker to mark the beginning of the round.

Knit 5 rounds to achieve a rolled edge.

Work "knit 2, purl 2" rib while working according to Chart A.

Change to size US 7 (4.5 mm) needle. Work 1 round while increasing (2, 0, 2) (0, 0, 0) (0, 0, 0) stitches evenly. You should now have (150, 160, 170) (180, 200, 220) (240, 260, 280) stitches. Place a second marker after (75, 80, 85) (90, 100, 110) (120, 130, 140) stitches to mark front and back sides.

Work pattern according to Chart B, starting where marked for selected size. The Chart will not go up in most sizes. Note: *By commencing at the marker, the pattern is positioned to ensure the seam appears invisible.* Continue until Body measures (14.2, 14.2, 15) (15.8, 16.6, 17.4) (17.4, 18.2, 18.2) in/(36, 36, 38) (40, 42, 44) (44, 46, 46) cm or desired length. From here you can either choose to knit the front piece and the back piece back and forth, or add 2 extra stitches between the front piece and the back piece for steeking. Continue in stockinette stitch until work measures (23.7, 23.7, 24.9) (25.7, 26.5, 26.5) (27.6, 28.4, 28.4) in/(60, 60, 63) (65, 67, 67) (70, 72, 72) cm or desired length. Place middle (45, 46, 45) (46, 48, 48) (50, 50, 50) stitches from the front piece and middle (45, 46, 45) (46, 48, 48) (50, 50, 50) stitches from the back piece on a needle.

The remaining stitches that form the shoulders are sewn together or Kitchener grafted at the end. Set the work aside and begin sleeves.

Sleeves

Cast on (36, 36, 40) (40, 40, 44) (44, 44, 44) stitches with C1 using size US 4 (3.5 mm) circular needle. Place a stitch marker to mark the beginning of the round. Knit 5 rounds to achieve a rolled edge.

Work "knit 2, purl 2" rib while working according to Chart A.

Change to US 7 (4.5 mm) size needle.

Work 1 round while increasing (14, 14, 10) (10, 10, 16) (16, 16, 16) stitches evenly.

You should now have (50, 50, 50) (50, 50, 60) (60, 60, 60) stitches. Work Chart B while increasing 2 stitches every 5th round (1 stitch after the first stitch of the round, and 1 stitch before the last st of the round) until you have (60, 60, 72) (72, 72, 84) (84, 96, 108) stitches. Let the increase go into the pattern. Continue in stockinette stitch until work measures (18.2, 19, 19.7) (21.3, 23, 23) (23.7, 23.7, 23.7) in/ (46, 48, 50) (54, 58, 58) (60, 60, 60) cm or desired length.

Turn the piece inside out and knit 3 rounds wrongside with C1 for covering over the cutting edge, if you choose to cut up to armhole. Bind off loosely. Knit the second sleeve like the first.

There are two options for the neck, high or short; follow the appropriate instructions below.

High Neck

Place middle (46, 45, 46) (45, 48, 48) (49, 50, 50) stitches from the front piece and middle (46, 45, 46) (45, 48, 48) (49, 50, 50) stitches from the back piece on size US 4 (3.5 mm) needle. You should now have (92, 90, 92) (90, 96, 96) (98, 100, 100) stitches. Knit 1 round and adjust the number of stitches (if needed) to (92, 92, 92) (92, 96, 96) (100, 100, 100) stitches.

Work "knit 2, purl 2" rib for 8 in (20 cm). Bind off loosely. Fold the neck.

Short Neck

Place middle (46, 45, 46) (45, 48, 48) (49, 50, 50) stitches from the front piece and middle (46, 45, 46) (45, 48, 48) (49, 50, 50) stitches from the back piece on size US 4 (3.5 mm) needle. You should now have (92, 90, 92) (90, 96, 96) (98, 100, 100) stitches. Knit 1 round and adjust the number of stitches (if needed) to (92, 92, 92) (92, 96, 96) (100, 100, 100) stitches.

Work "knit 2, purl 2" rib for 1.2 in (3 cm). Knit 5 rounds for a rolled edge. Bind off loosely.

Biboon
ÍSTEX Léttlopi
C1: 0051 White
C2: 1418 Straw
C3: 1419 Barley
C4: 9434 Crimson Red
C5: 9427 Rust
C6: 9431 Brick
C7: 1704 Apricot

Biboon
ÍSTEX Léttlopi
C1: 0051 White
C2: 0052 Black Sheep
C3: 0054 Ash
C4: 0056 Light Grey
C5: 0057 Grey
C6: 0085 Oatmeal
C7: 0086 Light Beige
C8: 1420 Murky

Finishing
Sew or Kitchener graft shoulders together.

If you choose to knit in a round: Sew two tight seams by hand or with a sewing machine corresponding to the width at the top of the sleeves, and then cut up between the seams. Set in sleeves.

If you choose to knit back and forth: Set in sleeves.

Afterward, weave in all ends, block the garment, and lay it flat to dry.

Chart A

X	X			12
X	X			11
X	X			10
X	X			9
X	X			8
X	X			7
X	X			6
X	X			5
X	X			4
X	X			3
X	X			2
X	X			1
4	3	2	1	

Chart B

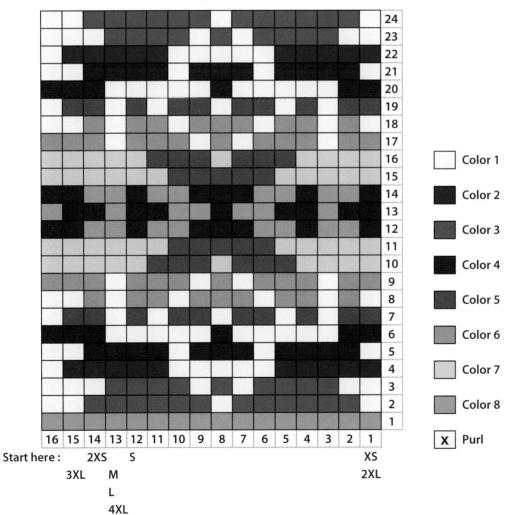

Color 1
Color 2
Color 3
Color 4
Color 5
Color 6
Color 7
Color 8
X   Purl

Start here :
2XS   S
3XL   M
L
4XL
XS
2XL

Haida

Haida, a project close to my heart, has finally become a reality.
It draws inspiration from my profound admiration for orcas.
Their intelligence, playful nature, and remarkable affection
have always captivated me.
One of my lifelong dreams is to have orcas swim alongside me while
kayaking. While that dream remains on hold for now, completing the
Haida sweater design brings me a sense of fulfillment.
I am excited to share this creation with you.

Haida

Starting with a ribbed hem, the body and sleeves are worked bottom up in the round and knit separately. A steek is added to the body for later arm attachment. The neck is knitted by picking up stitches from the body. The arms are knitted separately and sewn into the body afterwards.

Sizes
(2XS, XS, S) (M, L, XL) (2XL, 3XL, 4XL)

Recommended ease: 2–4 in (5–10 cm) positive ease

Measurements
Chest circumference:
Chest: (44.3, 50.6, 56.9) (60, 63.2, 69.5) (75.8, 82.2, 88.5) in/
(112, 128, 144) (152, 160, 176) (192, 208, 224) cm

Arm circumference:
(25.3, 25.3, 25.3) (25.3, 25.3, 80) (31.6, 31.6, 31.6) in/
(64, 64, 64) (64, 64, 80) (80, 80, 80) cm

Yarn
Brooklyn Tweed Quarry; bulky weight;
100% American Targhee-Columbia wool;
200 yd (183 m), 3.5 oz (100 g) per skein
Brooklyn Tweed Shelter (2 strands held together); worsted weight;
100% American Targhee-Columbia wool; 140 yd (128 m),
1.8 oz (50 g) per skein

C1 : Quarry – Woodsmoke: (5, 5, 6) (6, 6, 6) (7, 7, 7) skeins
C2: Quarry – Otter: (1, 1, 1) (2, 2, 2) (2, 2, 2) skeins
C3: Shelter – Long Johns: (2, 2, 2) (3, 3, 3) (4, 4, 4) skeins
C4: Quarry – Fossil: (0.5, 1, 1) (1, 1, 1) (1, 1.5, 1.5) skeins

Needles
Double-pointed needles: US 7 and US 10 (4.5 mm and 6 mm)
(unless the magic loop technique is used)
Circular needles, 16 in (40 cm): US 7 and US 10 (4.5 mm and 6 mm)
Circular needles, 32 in (80 cm): US 7 and US 10 (4.5 mm and 6 mm)

Gauge
14 stitches and 20 rows = 4 in (10 cm) on US 10 needle in stockinette stitch

Other
1 or 2 Buttons

Body

Cast on (112, 128, 144) (152, 160, 176) (192, 208, 224) stitches with C1 using size US 7 (4.5 mm) circular needle. Place a stitch marker to mark the beginning of the round and a second marker after (56, 64, 72) (76, 80, 88) (96, 104, 112) stitches to mark the front and back sides.

Work "knit 1, purl 1" rib for 2.75 in (7 cm). Change to size US 10 (6 mm) needle. Continue in stockinette stitch until work measures (15, 15.8, 15.8) (16.6, 16.6, 17.4) (17.4, 18.2, 18.2) in/(38, 40, 40) (42, 42, 44) (44, 46, 46) cm or desired length, allowing 9.8 in (25 cm) for Chart C. Follow Chart C until body measures (17, 17.8, 17.8) (18.6, 18.6, 19.3) (19.3, 20.1, 20.1) in/(43, 45, 45) (47, 47, 49) (49, 51, 51) cm.

From here you can choose to knit the front piece and the back piece back and forth, or to add 2 extra stitches in between the front piece and the back piece on each side if you prefer to knit in the round and cut (steek) the opening.

Continue knitting Chart C until row 41. Bind off 5 stitches in the middle of the front of the sweater. This will be the new beginning of the round. From here on, the yoke is knit back and forth in stockinette stitch. Finish the pattern and knit 3 more rows.

On a stitch holder set aside the middle (36, 36, 36) (40, 40, 40) (40, 44, 44) stitches ((+5 stitches) which are not included in the pattern) from the front piece and the middle (36, 36, 36) (40, 40, 40) (40, 44, 44) stitches from the back piece. The remaining stitches forming the shoulders are sewn together or Kitchener grafted at the end.

Hood

Place 1 stitch marker in the middle of the back. Knit back and forth in stockinette stitch until the hood measures 18.8 in (35 cm) or the desired length.
In the next 12 rounds, we will shape the top back side of the hood. The decreases take place on the left and right sides of the stitch marker placed at the back of the head. Decrease 1 stitch on each side of the marker every 2nd round, a total of 6 times (12 stitches decreased).

Graft the underarm stitches and the hood to close.

Hood Button Band

Pick up stitches for the button band as follows: Pick up 3 stitches, skip the 4th st, and repeat this pattern until you reach the other end of the hood.
Make sure to end up with an even number of stitches. Knit 1 row in stockinette stitch, then work the ribbing "knit 1, purl 1"
Repeat these rows until the button band measures 1.5 in (4 cm) on all sizes. If desired, knit buttonholes* on the left side of the hood; otherwise, skip this step for a hood without buttons.
Bind off and sew the bottom of the button band by laying the ends over each other.
Hide the steeked edges.

*Buttonholes: After 0.8 in (2 cm), knit 2 stitches together and then bind off 1 stitch. Binding off 1 stitch will fit well with 0.8–0.86 in (20–22 mm) buttons. Continue until button band measures 1.5 in (4 cm) on all sizes. Bind off more stitches if you want larger buttons.

Set the work aside and begin sleeves.

For a more detailed description in how to knit a Button band see page 58.

Sleeves

Cast on (32, 32, 32) (36, 36, 36) (40, 40, 40) stitches with C1 using size US 7 (4.5 mm) needle. Place a stitch marker to mark the start of the round.
Work "knit 1, purl 1" rib for 2.75 in (7 cm).
Change to size US 10 (6 mm) needle. Knit 1 round with C1, increasing (8, 8, 8) (4, 4, 4) (8, 8, 8) stitches evenly over the round. You should now have (40, 40, 40) (40, 40, 40) (48, 48, 48) stitches.
Work Chart A.
Continue in stockinette stitch increasing 2 stitches every 5th round (1 stitch after the first stitch of the round, and 1 stitch before the last stitch of the round) until you have (64, 64, 64) (64, 64, 80) (80, 80, 80) stitches or until work measures (14.2, 14.2, 14.6) (15.0, 15.4, 15.7) (15.7, 16.1, 16.1) in/(36, 36, 37) (38, 39, 40) (40, 41, 41) cm or desired length, allowing 4 in (10 cm) for Chart B.
Work pattern according to Chart B. Let increases run into the pattern if left.
Knit 3 more rounds in C2. Bind off loosely.
Knit the second sleeve like the first.

Finishing

Sew or Kitchener graft shoulders together.

If you choose to knit in a round: Sew two tight seams by hand or with a sewing machine corresponding to the width at the top of the sleeves, and then cut up between the seams. Set in sleeves.

If you choose to knit back and forth: Set in sleeves.

Afterward, add buttons, weave in all ends, block the garment, and lay it flat to dry.

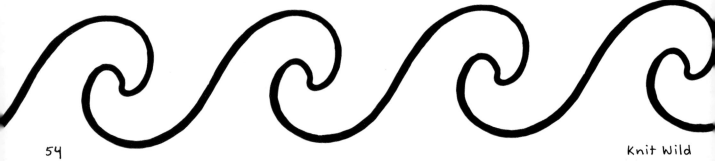

Knit Wild

Chart A

Chart B

Chart C

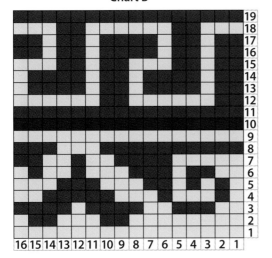

☐ Color 1
■ Color 2
■ Color 3
☐ Color 4

The Button Band

Knitting your first button band might seem overwhelming, so here is a more detailed explanation of the process.

To create a neat button band for your hoodie, pick up stitches along the edge, skipping every fourth stitch until you reach the other end. Make sure to end up with an even number of stitches for a clean button band look.

Knit the first row in stockinette stitch. After that, establish a ribbing pattern by alternating between purling one and knitting one on each row until the button band measures 1.5 inches (4 cm).

If you want buttons, create buttonholes on the left side starting after 0.8 inches (2 cm) of knitting. Do this by first knitting 2 stitches together and binding off 1 stitch, followed by casting on 1 stitch in the following round where we have bound off to create a little hole. Adjust the number of stitches bound off based on the size of your buttons. Continue the ribbing for an additional 0.8 inches (2 cm).

Finally, bind off and sew the bottom of the button band by laying the ends over each other to achieve a folded look.

To conceal the seam inside the hood, pick up stitches along the steek, skipping every fourth stitch until you reach the other end. Knit 2 cm in stockinette stitch and fold over the seam. Sew it in place. This technique is also called a Steek Sandwich.

Instead of the Steek Sandwich, you can use a ribbon to hide the seam. Pin a ribbon into place over right front steek, beginning at the bottom edge of the button band, turning under top and bottom edges to neaten, and overlapping neck band ribbon to finish. Sew into place using a small slip stitch all around the ribbon.

Zion

Zion is named and designed after the Zion National Park.
When I envision winters in the park, I see the sun shining brightly on the rugged
rocks, casting mesmerizing patterns over the sprawling mountains. Nature is
delicately adorned with a gentle layer of snow, creating a serene and beautiful
landscape. The design of Zion reflects the breathtaking beauty of the Zion
National Park, capturing its essence in every stitch

Zion

This pattern is worked seamlessly in the round from the bottom up. First, the body and sleeves are worked up separately. Then, the body and arms are joined to form the yoke, which is worked in the round on a circular needle and shaped with decreases. The sweater is finished with a turtleneck.

Sizes
(2XS, XS, S) (M, L, XL) (2XL, 3XL, 4XL)

Measurements
Chest Circumference:
(36.6, 36.6, 38.6) (43.3, 46.1, 50.8) (53.5, 58.3, 63) in/
(93, 93, 98) (110, 117, 129) (136, 148, 160) cm
Arm circumference:
(18.1, 18.1, 18.1) (18.9, 18.9, 19.7) (19.7, 20.1, 20.5) in/
(46, 46, 46) (48, 48, 50) (50, 51, 52) cm

Yarn
Ístex Álafosslopi; bulky weight; 100% new Icelandic wool; 109 yd
(99.5 m), 3.5 oz (100 g) per skein

Rauma Vams; bulky weight; 100% new Norwegian wool; 90 yd
(83 m), 1.8 oz (50 g) per skein

C1: Álafosslopi—0086 Light Beige: (4, 5, 5) (5, 6, 6) (6, 7, 7) skeins
C2: Vams—47 Petrol: (2, 2, 2) (3, 3, 3) (4, 4, 4) skeins
C3: Vams—50 Light Blue Jeans: (2, 2, 2) (3, 3, 3) (4, 4, 4) skeins

Needles
Double-pointed needles: US 7 and US 10 (4.5 mm and 6 mm)
(unless the magic loop technique is used)
Circular needles, 16 in (40 cm): US 7 and US 10 (4.5 mm and 6 mm)
Circular needles, 32 in (80 cm): US 7 and US 10 (4.5 mm and 6 mm)

Gauge
14 stitches and 20 rows = 4 in (10 cm) on US 10 needle in
stockinette stitch

Body

Cast on (90, 100, 120) (140, 160, 180) (200, 220, 240) stitches with C1 using size US 7 (4.5 mm) circular needle. Place a stitch marker to mark the beginning of the round and after (45, 50, 60) (70, 80, 90) (100, 110, 120) stitches to mark the front and back pieces.

Work "knit 1, purl 1" rib for 3 in (7.5 cm).

Change to a US 10 (6 mm) circular needle. Continue in stockinette stitch until work measures (12.6, 12.6, 12.6) (13.4, 14.2, 15.0) (15.0, 15.0, 15.7) in/(32, 32, 32) (34, 36, 38) (38, 38, 40) cm or desired length, allowing 4 in (10 cm) for Chart B.

Work Chart B.

Place the first (5, 5, 5) (5, 10, 10) (10, 15, 15) stitches of the round on a holder or waste yarn. The stitches for the other armhole will be put on holder when you start the yoke. Set the work aside and begin sleeves.

Sleeves

Cast on (36, 36, 36) (36, 42, 42) (42, 48, 48) stitches with C1 using size US 7 (4.5 mm) circular needle. Place a stitch marker to mark the beginning of the round.

Work "knit 1, purl 1" rib for 3 in (7.5 cm).

Change to size US 10 (6 mm) circular needle. Knit 1 round in C1.

Work pattern according to Chart A.

Continue in stockinette stitch increasing 2 stitches every 5th round (1 stitch after the first stitch of the round, and 1 stitch before the last st of the round) until you have (60, 60, 60) (60, 70, 70) (70, 80, 80) stitches.

Continue in stockinette stitch until work measures (14.2, 14.2, 14.6) (15.0, 15.4, 15.7) (15.7, 16.1, 16.1) in/(36, 36, 37) (38, 39, 40) (40, 41, 41) cm or desired length, allowing 4 in (10 cm) for Chart B.

Work Chart B.

Place the first (5, 5, 5) (5, 10, 10) (10, 15, 15) stitches of the round on a stitch holder or waste yarn. It is crucial that these first 5 stitches are set aside because they are essential for the proper alignment of the charts when you join the round.

Knit the second sleeve like the first.

Yoke

Join body and sleeves on a US 10 (6 mm) circular needle. Place a stitch marker to mark the beginning of the round at the first join.

Knit over first sleeve.

Work the front piece (40, 40, 50) (60, 60, 70) (80, 80, 90) stitches. Transfer next (5, 5, 5) (5, 10, 10) (10, 15, 15) stitches onto a stitch holder or waste yarn for underarm. Knit over the other sleeve and back piece. You should now have (190, 200, 220) (240, 260, 280) (300, 320, 340) stitches.

Work pattern according to Chart C and decrease as directed. Change to shorter needle when necessary. After completing chart (76, 80, 88) (96, 104, 112) (120, 128, 136) stitches remain on needles.

Knit 1 round in C2 while decreasing (20, 16, 16) (16, 16, 16) (16, 16, 16) stitches evenly over the round. You should now have (56, 64, 72) (80, 88, 96) (104, 112, 120) stitches remaining on needles.

Knit Chart D.

Neck

Change to size US 7 (4.5 mm) needle. Knit 1 round with C1, decreasing (0, 0, 0) (4, 8, 12) (20, 24, 28) stitches evenly over the round. You should now have (56, 64, 72) (76, 80, 84) (84, 88, 92) stitches on needles.

Work "knit 2, purl 2" rib for 8 in (20 cm). Bind off loosely.

Finishing

Graft the underarm stitches to close, then weave in all ends. Block the garment and lay it flat to dry. Finally, fold the neck.

Zion

Zion
BROOKLYN TWEED Quarry +
SPINCYLE YARNS Plump
C1: Quarry Otter
C2: Quarry Fossil
C3: Plump MISS ME

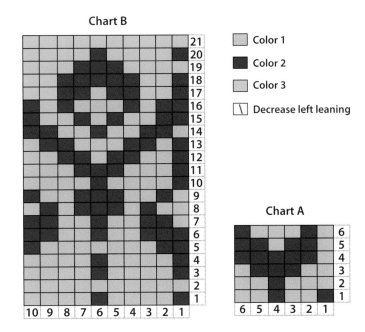

Chart B

Color 1
Color 2
Color 3
Decrease left leaning

Chart A

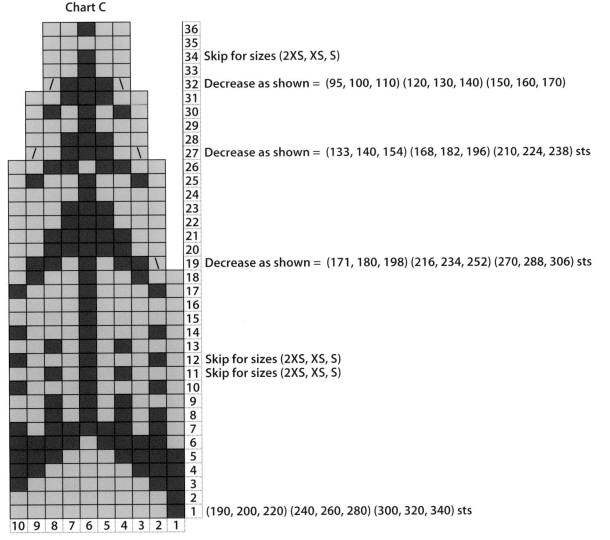

Chart D

Chart C

36
35
34 Skip for sizes (2XS, XS, S)
33
32 Decrease as shown = (95, 100, 110) (120, 130, 140) (150, 160, 170)
31
30
29
28
27 Decrease as shown = (133, 140, 154) (168, 182, 196) (210, 224, 238) sts
26
25
24
23
22
21
20
19 Decrease as shown = (171, 180, 198) (216, 234, 252) (270, 288, 306) sts
18
17
16
15
14
13
12 Skip for sizes (2XS, XS, S)
11 Skip for sizes (2XS, XS, S)
10
9
8
7
6
5
4
3
2
1 (190, 200, 220) (240, 260, 280) (300, 320, 340) sts

Zion

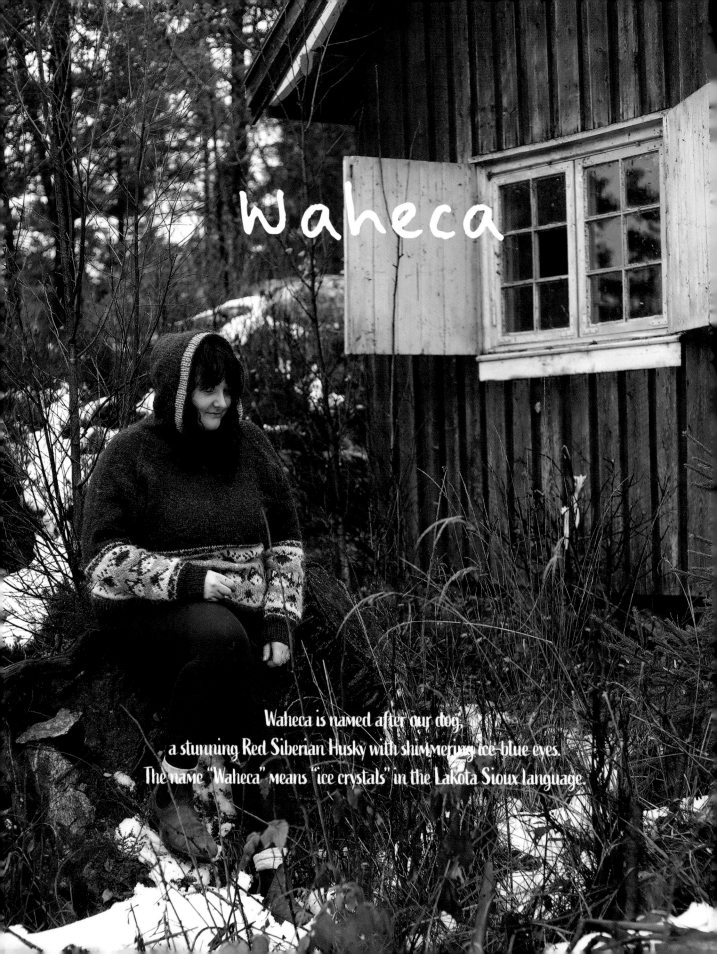

Waheca

Waheca is named after our dog,
a stunning Red Siberian Husky with shimmering ice-blue eyes.
The name "Waheca" means "ice crystals" in the Lakota Sioux language.

Waheca

This pattern is worked seamlessly in the round from the bottom up. First, the body and sleeves are worked up separately. Then, the body and arms are joined to form the yoke, which is worked in the round on a circular needle and shaped with decreases to achieve a raglan fit. The sweater is finished with your choice of high neck, turtleneck, or hood.

Sizes
(2XS, XS, S) (M, L, XL) (2XL, 3XL, 4XL)

Recommended ease: 4 in (10 cm) positive ease

Measurements
Chest circumference:
(31.2, 34, 37.1) (40.3, 43.8, 47.4) (50.1, 54.1, 57.6) in/
(78, 86, 94) (102, 111, 120) (129, 137, 146) cm

Arm circumference:
(14.6, 15.4, 15.8) (16.2, 17, 17.4) (18.2, 18.6, 19.3) in/
(37, 39, 40) (41, 43, 44) (46, 47, 49) cm

Yarn
Ístex Álafosslopi; bulky weight; 100% new Icelandic wool;
109 yd (99.5 m), 3.5 oz (100 g) per skein

C1: 9961 Bordeaux: (5, 5, 5.5) (5.5, 6, 6) (6.5, 6.5, 7) skeins
C2: 9964 Golden: (1, 1, 1) (1.5, 1.5, 1.5) (2, 2, 2) skeins
C3: 0867 Chocolate: (1, 1, 1) (1.5, 1.5, 1.5) (2, 2, 2) skeins
C4: 0051 White: (0.5, 1, 1) (1, 1, 1) (1, 1.5, 1.5) skeins

Needles
Double-pointed needles: US 7 and US 10 (4.5 mm and 6 mm)
(unless the magic loop technique is used)
Circular needles, 16 in (40 cm): US 7 and US 10 (4.5 mm and 6 mm)
Circular needles, 32 in (80 cm): US 7 and US 10 (4.5 mm and 6 mm)

Gauge
14 stitches and 20 rows = 4 in (10 cm) on US 10 needle in
stockinette stitch

Other
1 or 2 Buttons

Body

Cast on (108, 120, 132) (144, 156, 168) (180, 192, 204) stitches with C1 using size US 7 (4.5 mm) circular needle. Place a stitch marker to mark the beginning of the round and a second marker after (52, 60, 66) (72, 78, 84) (90, 96, 102) stitches to mark the front and back sides.

Work "knit 1, purl 1" rib for 3 in (7.5 cm).

Change to a US 10 (6 mm) circular needle. Knit 1 round in C1.

Knit Chart A.

Continue in stockinette stitch until work measures (18, 18.5, 19.25) (19.5, 19.75, 20) (20.5, 20.75, 21.25) in/(46, 47, 48) (49, 50, 51) (52, 53, 54) cm or desired length.

Place the first (3, 3, 4) (4, 5, 5) (6, 6, 7) stitches of the beginning of the round and the last (2, 3, 3) (4, 4, 5) (5, 6, 6) stitches onto a stitch holder or waste yarn for underarm, a total of (5, 6, 7) (8, 9, 10) (11, 12, 13) stitches. Set the work aside and begin sleeves.

Sleeves

Cast on (36, 36, 36) (38, 38, 38) (42, 42, 42) stitches with C1 using size US 7 (4.5 mm) circular needle. Place a stitch marker to mark the beginning of the round.

Work "knit 1, purl 1" rib for 3 in (7.5 cm).

Change to a US 10 (6 mm) circular needle. Knit 1 round in C1 and increase (0, 0, 0) (10, 10, 10) (6, 6, 6) stitches over the round. You should now have (36, 36, 36) (48, 48, 48) (48, 48, 48) stitches on needles.

Knit Chart A while increasing 2 stitches every 5th round (1 stitch after the first stitch of the round, and 1 stitch before the last st of the round) until you have (52, 54, 56) (58, 60, 62) (64, 66, 68) stitches.

Continue in stockinette stitch until work measures (18.25, 18.25, 18.5) (18.75, 19.25, 19.75) (19.75, 20, 20) in/(46, 46, 47) (48, 49, 50) (50, 51, 51) cm or desired length. Place the first (3, 3, 4) (4, 5, 5) (6, 6, 7) stitches of the beginning of a round and the last (2, 3, 3) (4, 4, 5) (5, 6, 6) stitches onto a stitch holder or waste yarn for underarm, a total of (5, 6, 7) (8, 9, 10) (11, 12, 13) stitches.

Knit the second sleeve like the first.

Yoke

Join body and sleeves on size US 10 (6 mm) circular needle. Place a stitch marker between every joining piece. Place an additional stitch marker at the first join to mark the start of the round = 4 (+1) markers placed. Knit over first sleeve. Knit the front. Knit over the other sleeve and back. You should now have (192, 204, 216) (228, 240, 252) (264, 276, 288) stitches.

Knit first (0.4, 0.4, 0.4) (0.6, 0.6, 0.8) (0.8, 1.2, 1.2) in/ (1, 1, 1) (1.5, 1.5, 2) (2, 3, 3) cm in stockinette stitch.

From here, we will shape the raglan.

Raglan Decrease: On each side of the marked stitches, decrease 1 stitch to the left and 1 stitch to the right (2 stitches per join), a total of 8 stitches decreased per round every 2nd round. On the right side of the marker, decrease by knitting 2 stitches together through the back loops. On the left side of the marker, decrease by knitting 2 stitches together. Change to a shorter circular needle if necessary. Work to (6.3, 6.7, 7.1) (7.5, 7.9, 8.3) (8.7, 9.1, 9.4) in/(16, 17, 18) (19, 20, 21) (22, 23, 24) cm from the joining edge.

Decide if you want to knit a hoodie, high neck, or turtleneck and follow the appropriate instructions below.

High Neck

Repeat decrease every other round and knit 2 in (5 cm) more or until (64, 68, 72) (68, 72, 76) (72, 76, 80) stitches remain on needles.

Knit 1 round and decrease to (64, 64, 68) (68, 68, 68) (72, 72, 76) stitches.

Change to size US 7 (4.5 mm) circular needle. Work "knit 2, purl 2" rib for 3 in (7.5 cm). Bind off loosely.

Turtleneck

Repeat decrease every other round and knit 2 in (5 cm) more or until (64, 68, 72) (68, 72, 76) (72, 76, 80) stitches remain on needles.

Change to size US 7 (4.5 mm) circular needle. Work "knit 2, purl 2" rib for 8 in (20 cm). Bind off loosely.

Hood

Bind off 5 stitches in the middle of the front of the sweater. This will be the new beginning of the round. From here on, the yoke is knit back and forth. Repeat Raglan decrease every other round and knit 2 in (5 cm) more or until (64, 68, 72) (68, 72, 76) (72, 76, 80) stitches remain on needles.

Knit 1 round and decrease to (64, 64, 64) (68, 68, 68) (72, 72, 72) stitches. Place 1 stitch marker in the middle of the back.

Knit back and forth in stockinette stitch until the hood measures 18.8 in (35 cm) or the desired length. In the next 12 rounds, we will shape the top back side of the hood. The decreases take place on the left and right sides of the stitch marker placed at the back of the head. Decrease 1 stitch on each side of the marker every 2nd round, a total of 6 times (12 stitches decreased).

Graft the underarm stitches and the hood to close.

Hood Button Band

Pick up stitches for the button band as follows: Pick up 3 stitches, skip the 4th st, and repeat this pattern until you reach the other end of the hood. Make sure to end up with an even number of stitches.

Knit 1 row in stockinette stitch, then work the ribbing as follows:

Row 1: Purl 1, knit 1.
Row 2: Knit 1, purl 1.

Repeat these rows until the button band measures 1.5 in (4 cm) on all sizes. If desired, knit buttonholes* on the left side of the hood; otherwise, skip this step for a hood without buttons.

Bind off in a contrasting color and sew the bottom of the button band by laying it over each other. Hide the steeked edges.

*Buttonholes: After 0.8 in (2 cm), knit 2 stitches together and then bind off 1 stitch. Binding off 1 stitch will fit well with 0.8–0.86 in (20–22 mm) buttons. Bind off more stitches if you want larger buttons.

For a more detailed description in how to knit a Buttonband see page 58.

Finishing

Graft the underarm stitches to close, then weave in all ends. Afterward, add buttons, block the garment, and lay it flat to dry.

Chart

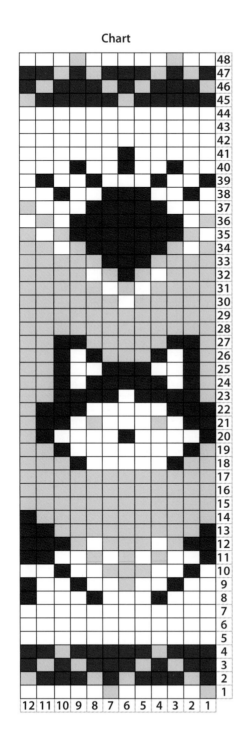

Color 1

Color 2

Color 3

Color 4

Denali

Denali is the highest peak of North America and is one of the most iconic and majestic mountains in the world. It is located in Denali National Park and Preserve in the state of Alaska, USA. The mountain was originally called "Denali" by the Koyukon Athabaskan people and it means "The High One" or "The Great One." Inspired by the majestic Alaskan mountains, this sweater design captures the essence of one of my favorite places on Earth. It took time and careful consideration to choose a name that truly honors the wild spirit of this design, and Denali proved to be the perfect choice.

The Denali sweater is a simple design and the word Denali may sound like a simple name but for me it stands for harsh weather conditions, strong winds, extremely cold temperatures, and frequent storms. It stands for diverse wildlife, including grizzly bears, moose, caribou, wolves, and Dall sheep.

Denali

Holding 2 strands together this pattern is worked seamlessly from the bottom up, starting with a ribbed hem and ending with a ribbed neck. The body and sleeves are worked bottom up and then joined to work the yoke in a raglan shape. The sweater can be knitted with a turtle-neck or a comfortable long neck.

Sizes
(2XS, XS, S) (M, L, XL) (2XL, 3XL, 4XL)

Recommended ease: 2–4 in (5–10 cm) positive ease

Measurements
Chest circumference:
(34, 37, 39.5) (42.3, 45, 47.8) (50.6, 53.3, 56.5) in/
(86, 93, 100) (107, 114, 121) (128, 135, 143) cm

Arm circumference:
(15, 15.4, 15.8) (16.6, 17.4, 17.8) (18.6, 19.4, 20.2) in/
(38, 39, 40) (42, 44, 45) (47, 49, 51) cm

Yarn
Kelbourne Woolens Andorra; (2 strands of held together);
sport weight; 60% Merino wool/20% Highland wool; 20% mohair;
185 yd (169 m), 1.8 oz (50 g) per skein

Version 1:
C1: 223 Mushroom: (4, 4, 5) (5, 5, 6) (6, 7, 7) skeins
C2: 105 Snow White: (2, 2, 2) (2, 2, 2) (2, 2, 2) skeins
C3: 306 Avocado: (1, 1, 1) (1, 1, 1) (1, 1, 1) skeins

Version 2:
C1: 105 Snow White: (4, 4, 5) (5, 5, 6) (6, 7, 7) skeins
C2: 613 Holly Red: (2, 2, 2) (2, 2, 2) (2, 2, 2) skeins
C3: 665 Salmon Pink: (1, 1, 1) (1, 1, 1) (1, 1, 1) skeins

Needles
Double-pointed needles: US 7 and US 10 (4.5 mm and 6 mm)
(unless the magic loop technique is used)
Circular needles, 16 in (40 cm): US 7 and US 10 (4.5 mm and 6 mm)
Circular needles, 32 in (80 cm): US 7 and US 10 (4.5 mm and 6 mm)

Gauge
14 stitches and 20 rounds = 4 in (10 cm)
on US 10 needles in stockinette stitch

Body

Cast on (120, 130, 140) (150, 160, 170) (180, 190, 200) stitches with C1 using size US 7 (4.5 mm) circular needle. Place a stitch marker to mark the beginning of the round and a second marker after (60, 65, 70) (75, 80, 85) (90, 95, 100) stitches to mark the front and back pieces.

Work "knit 1, purl 2" rib for 0.8 in (2 cm).

Change to size US 10 (6 mm) circular needle. Work Chart A.

Continue in stockinette stitch until work measures (18, 18.5, 19.25) (19.5, 19.75, 20) (20.5, 20.75, 21.25) in/(46, 47, 48) (49, 50, 51) (52, 53, 54) cm or desired length. Place first (3, 3, 3) (3, 4, 4) (4, 5, 5) stitches and last (3, 3, 3) (4, 4, 4) (5, 5, 6) stitches onto a stitch holder or waste yarn for underarm, a total of (6, 6, 6) (7, 8, 8) (9, 10, 11) stitches. The stitches for the other armhole will be put on holder when you start the yoke.

Set the work aside and begin sleeves.

Sleeves

Cast on (32, 34, 34) (36, 36, 38) (38, 40, 40) stitches with C1 using size US 7 (4.5 mm) circular needle. Place a stitch marker to mark the beginning of the round.

Work "knit 1, purl 2" rib for 0.8 in (2 cm).

Change to size US 10 (6 mm) circular needle. Work Chart A.

Continue in stockinette stitch increasing 2 stitches every 5th round (1 stitch after the first stitch of the round and 1 stitch before the last st of the round) until you have (54, 55, 56) (59, 62, 63) (66, 69, 72) stitches. Continue in stockinette stitch until work measures (18.25, 18.25, 18.5) (18.75, 19.25, 19.75) (19.75, 20, 20) in/(46, 46, 47) (48, 49, 50) (50, 51, 51) cm or desired length.

Place first (3, 3, 3) (3, 4, 4) (4, 5, 5) stitches and last (3, 3, 3) (4, 4, 4) (5, 5, 6) stitches onto a stitch holder or waste yarn for underarm, a total of (6, 6, 6) (7, 8, 8) (9, 10, 11) stitches.

Knit the second sleeve like the first.

Yoke

Join body and sleeves on size US 10 (6 mm) circular needle. Place a stitch marker between every joining piece. Place an additional stitch marker at the first join to mark the start of the round = 4 (+1) markers placed. Knit over first sleeve. Knit the front. Knit over the other sleeve and back. You should now have (204, 216, 228) (240, 252, 264) (276, 288, 300) stitches. Knit (3, 3, 4) (5, 6, 7) (8, 9, 10) rounds in stockinette stitch.

From here, we will shape the raglan.

Knit Chart B followed by Chart C while shaping the raglan. Work Chart B heightwise once, then work Chart C continuously until the neck. The stitches directly to the left and right of the marked stitches are always knit in C1.

Raglan Decrease: On each side of the marked stitches, decrease 1 stitch to the left and 1 stitch to the right (2 stitches per join), a total of 8 stitches decreased per round every 2nd round. On the right side of marker, decrease by knitting 2 stitches together through the back loops of the stitches. On the left side of the marker, decrease by knitting 2 stitches together. Change to a shorter circular needle if necessary.

Repeat decrease every other round until you have (84, 88, 92) (96, 100, 104) (108, 112, 116) stitches left.

Knit 1 round and decrease (4, 8, 6) (12, 12, 16) (16, 20, 20) stitches evenly over the round. You should now have (80, 80, 84) (84, 88, 88) (92, 92, 96) stitches on the needles.

Decide if you want to knit a long neck or turtleneck and follow the appropriate instructions.

Long Neck
Work "knit 2, purl 2" rib for 3 in (7.5 cm). Bind off loosely.

Turtleneck
Work "knit 2, purl 2" rib for 8 in (20 cm). Bind off loosely.

Finishing
Graft the underarm stitches to close, then weave in all ends. Block the garment and lay it flat to dry. Finally, fold the neck.

Version 1

Chart A

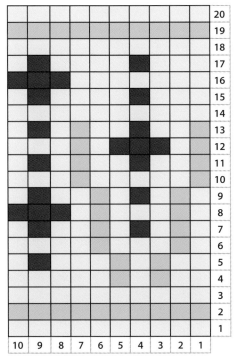

Chart B

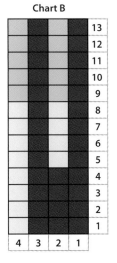

Color 1

Color 2

Color 3

Chart C

Version 2

Chart A

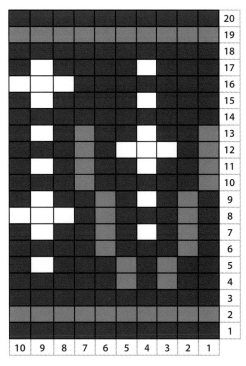

Chart B

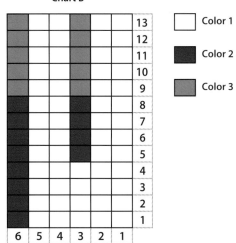

Color 1

Color 2

Color 3

Chart C

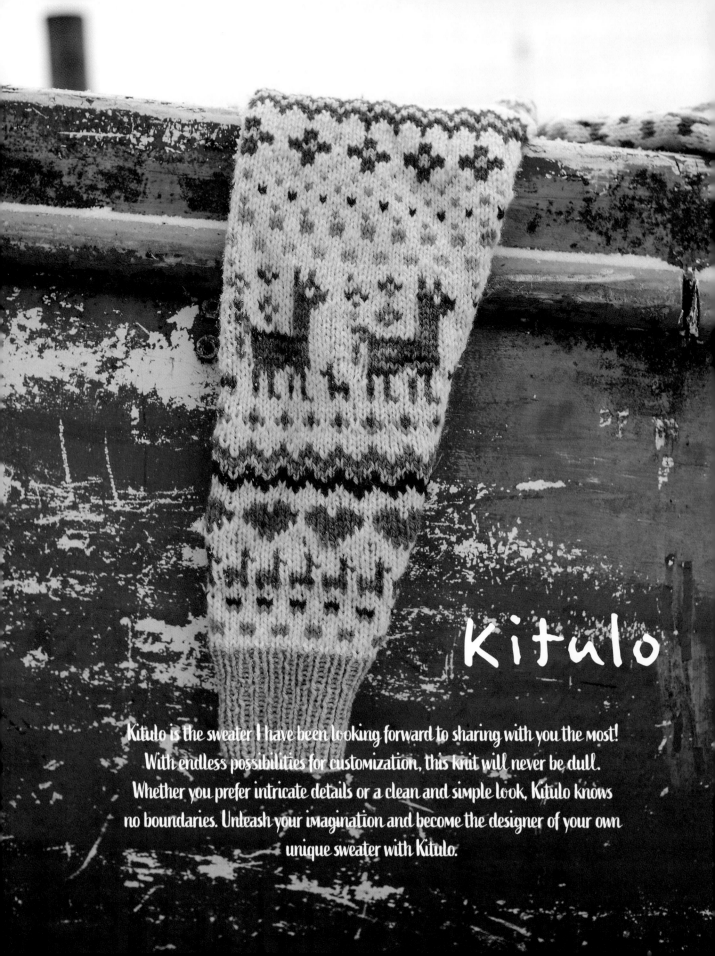

Kitulo

Kitulo is the sweater I have been looking forward to sharing with you the most!
With endless possibilities for customization, this knit will never be dull.
Whether you prefer intricate details or a clean and simple look, Kitulo knows
no boundaries. Unleash your imagination and become the designer of your own
unique sweater with Kitulo.

Kitulo

This pattern is worked seamlessly from the bottom up, starting with a ribbed hem and ending with a ribbed neck. The body and sleeves are worked bottom up and then joined to work the yoke. All numbers are given and it is up to you to choose how you would like to place the charts.

Sizes
(2XS, XS, S) (M, L, XL) (2XL, 3XL, 4XL)

Recommended ease: 2–4 in (5–10 cm) positive ease

Measurements
Chest circumference:
(36, 39.75, 43) (46.5, 49.5, 53) (56.5, 59.5, 63) in/
(92, 101, 109) (118, 126, 136) (143, 151, 160) cm

Arm circumference:
(13.25, 14, 15) (15.75, 16.5, 17.25) (18, 18.75, 19.5) in/
(34, 36, 38) (40, 42, 44) (46, 48, 50) cm

Yarn
Brooklyn Tweed Shelter; worsted weight; 100% American Targhee-Columbia wool; 140 yd (128 m),
1.8 oz (50 g) per skein
Brooklyn Tweed Tones; worsted weight; 100% American Columbia wool; 140 yd (128 m),
1.8 oz (50 g) per skein

Main Color: Shelter – Fossil: (8, 8, 8) (10, 10, 10) (12, 12, 12) skeins
C2: Tones – Persimmon Overtone: (2, 2, 2) (2, 2, 2) (2, 2, 2) skeins
C3: Tones – Goldfinch Overtone: (2, 2, 2) (2, 2, 2) (2, 2, 2) skeins
C4: Tones – Melba Overtone: (2, 2, 2) (2, 2, 2) (2, 2, 2) skeins
C5: Tones – Vacay Overtone: (2, 2, 2) (2, 2, 2) (2, 2, 2) skeins
C6: Tones – Granita Overtone: (2, 2, 2) (2, 2, 2) (2, 2, 2) skeins
C7: Shelter – Long Johns: (2, 2, 2) (2, 2, 2) (2, 2, 2) skeins
I am using the Charts A, B, E, G, H, J, P, U, X, Y and Z in this Sample.

Please take note: The quantity of yarn required is entirely reliant on your individual design choices for your sweater. *To estimate how much yarn you will need: knit a small sample, wash and smooth it out, measure its size, weigh it, and then calculate how many grams you used for each square inch (or square centimeter). Once you have this ratio, use it to estimate the amount of yarn you will need for your whole sweater.*

Needles
Double-pointed needles: US 4 and US 6 (3.5 mm and 4 mm) (unless the magic loop technique is used)
Circular needles, 16 in (40 cm): US 4 and US 6 (3.5 mm and 4 mm)
Circular needles, 32 in (80 cm): US 4 and US 6 (3.5 mm and 4 mm)

Gauge
19 stitches and 28 rows = 4 in (10 cm) on US 6 needle in stockinette stitch

Body

Cast on (176, 192, 208) (224, 240, 256) (272, 288, 304) stitches with Main Color using size US 4 (3.5 mm) circular needle. Place a stitch marker at the beginning of the round and a second marker after (88, 96, 104) (112, 120, 128) (136, 144, 152) stitches to mark the front and back sides.

Work "knit1, purl 1" rib for 2.75 in (7 cm).

Change to size US 6 (4 mm) needle. Continue in stockinette stitch until work measures (18, 18.5, 19.25) (19.5, 19.75, 20) (20.5, 20.75, 21.25) in/(46, 47, 48) (49, 50, 51) (52, 53, 54) cm or desired length. Place (4, 5, 6) (7, 8, 9) (10, 11, 12) stitches at the beginning of a round and the last (4, 5, 6) (7, 8, 9) (10, 11, 12) stitches onto a stitch holder or waste yarn for underarm, a total of (8, 10, 12) (14, 16, 18) (20, 22, 24) stitches. Set the work aside and begin sleeves.

Sleeves

Cast on (36, 38, 40) (40, 42, 42) (38, 40, 40) stitches with Main Color using size US 4 (3.5 mm) circular needle. Place a stitch marker to mark the beginning of the round.

Work "knit 1, purl 1" rib for 2.75 in (7 cm).

Change to US 6 (4 mm) size needle. Continue in stockinette stitch increasing 2 stitches every 5th round (1 stitch after the first stitch of the round, and 1 stitch before the last st of the round) until you have (64, 68, 72) (76, 80, 84) (88, 92, 96) stitches.

Continue in stockinette stitch until work measures (18.25, 18.25, 18.5) (18.75, 19.25, 19.75) (19.75, 20, 20) in/(46, 46, 47) (48, 49, 50) (50, 51, 51) cm. Place (4, 5, 6) (7, 8, 9) (10, 11, 12) stitches at the beginning of a round and the last (4, 5, 6) (7, 8, 9) (10, 11, 12) stitches onto a stitch holder or waste yarn for underarm, a total of (8, 10, 12) (14, 16, 18) (20, 22, 24) stitches.

Knit the second sleeve like the first.

Yoke

Join body and sleeves on size US 6 (4 mm) circular needle. Place a stitch marker to mark the beginning of the round at the first join. Knit over first sleeve.

Work the front, transfer next (6, 8, 10) (12, 14, 16) (18, 20, 22) stitches onto a stitch holder or waste yarn for underarm. Knit over the other sleeve and back. You should now have (272, 288, 304) (320, 336, 352) (368, 384, 400) stitches.

Work pattern according to the charts and decrease according to the size you are knitting, as below.

Note! Always decrease in the first row of a new chart.

For example:
The pattern suggests to decrease at round 22 however your chosen chart doesn't end until row 24. Decrease at round 25 instead. If your chart ends at row 20. Decrease at row 21 instead.

2XS – 272 stitches: Chart total length: 42 rounds.
Round 22: Decrease 48 stitches evenly over the round = 224 stitches
Round 30: Decrease 56 stitches evenly over the round = 168 stitches
Round 38: Decrease 48 stitches evenly over the round = 120 stitches
Round 42: Decrease 36 stitches evenly over the round = 84 stitches

XS – 288 stitches: Chart total length: 42 rounds.
Round 22: Decrease 48 stitches evenly over the round = 240 stitches
Round 30: Decrease 64 stitches evenly over the round = 160 stitches
Round 38: Decrease 48 stitches evenly over the round = 128 stitches
Round 42: Decrease 40 stitches evenly over the round = 88 stitches

S – 304 stitches: Chart total length: 46 rounds.
Round 22: Decrease 48 stitches evenly over the round = 256 stitches
Round 30: Decrease 48 stitches evenly over the round = 208 stitches
Round 38: Decrease 48 stitches evenly over the round = 160 stitches
Round 46: Decrease 48 stitches evenly over the round = 92 stitches

M – 320 stitches: Chart total length: 46 rounds.
Round 22: Decrease 48 stitches evenly over the round = 272 stitches.
Round 30: Decrease 64 stitches evenly over the round = 208 stitches.
Round 38: Decrease 56 stitches evenly over the round = 152 stitches.
Round 46: Decrease 56 stitches evenly over the round = 96 stitches.

L – 336 stitches: Chart total length: 52 rounds.
Round 22: Decrease 64 stitches evenly over the round = 272 stitches
Round 30: Decrease 48 stitches evenly over the round = 224 stitches
Round 38: Decrease 48 stitches evenly over the round = 176 stitches
Round 46: Decrease 36 stitches evenly over the round = 140 stitches
Round 52: Decrease 32 stitches evenly over the round = 104 stitches

XL – 352 stitches: Chart total length: 52 rounds.
Round 22: Decrease 64 stitches evenly over the round = 288 stitches
Round 30: Decrease 64 stitches evenly over the round = 224 stitches
Round 38: Decrease 48 stitches evenly over the round = 176 stitches
Round 46: Decrease 40 stitches evenly over the round = 136 stitches
Round 52: Decrease 28 stitches evenly over the round = 108 stitches

2XL – 368 stitches: Chart total length: 52 rounds.
Round 22: Decrease 64 stitches evenly over the round = 304 stitches
Round 30: Decrease 64 stitches evenly over the round = 240 stitches
Round 38: Decrease 64 stitches evenly over the round = 176 stitches
Round 46: Decrease 32 stitches evenly over the round = 144 stitches
Round 52: Decrease 32 stitches evenly over the round = 112 stitches

3XL – 384 stitches: Chart total length: 56 rounds.
Round 22: Decrease 80 stitches evenly over the round = 304 stitches
Round 30: Decrease 42 stitches evenly over the round = 262 stitches
Round 38: Decrease 42 stitches evenly over the round = 220 stitches
Round 46: Decrease 42 stitches evenly over the round = 178 stitches
Round 52: Decrease 42 stitches evenly over the round = 136 stitches
Round 56: Decrease 20 stitches evenly over the round = 116 stitches

4XL – 400 stitches: Chart total length: 56 rounds.
Round 22: Decrease 80 stitches evenly over the round = 320 stitches
Round 30: Decrease 44 stitches evenly over the round = 276 stitches
Round 38: Decrease 44 stitches evenly over the round = 232 stitches
Round 46: Decrease 44 stitches evenly over the round = 188 stitches
Round 52: Decrease 44 stitches evenly over the round = 144 stitches
Round 56: Decrease 24 stitches evenly over the round = 120 stitches

Change to shorter needle when necessary. After completing chart (84, 88, 92) (96, 104, 108) (112, 116, 120) stitches remain on needles.

Choose from short neck, rolled neck, or turtleneck and follow instructions below.

Short Neck
Work "knit 1, purl 1" rib for 3 in (7.5 cm). Bind off loosely.

Rolled Neck
Knit 5 rounds to achieve a rolled edge. Bind off loosely.

Turtleneck
Work "knit 2, purl 2" rib for 8 in (20 cm). Bind off loosely.

Finishing
Graft the underarm stitches to close, then weave in all ends. Block the garment and lay it flat to dry. Finally, fold the neck.

The Charts Used in the Main Sample:

Charts are listed from the bottom up.

Body
Z, G, P, X, H, E, J, F, B, U

Sleeves
F, C, H, P, A, Z, F, E, J, P, U, B, A

Yoke
Y, F, H, B, A

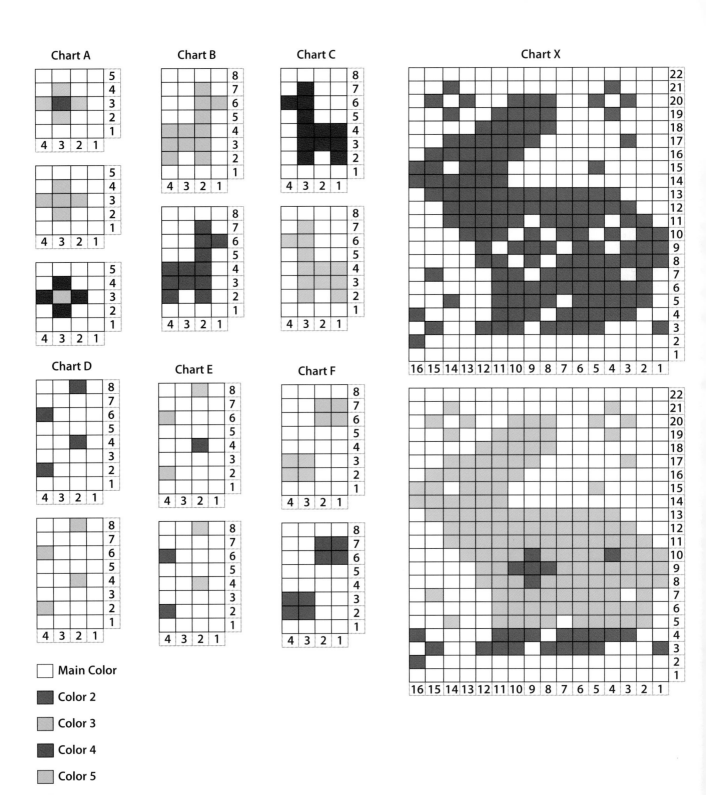

Chart A

Chart B

Chart C

Chart X

Chart D

Chart E

Chart F

☐ Main Color

■ Color 2

☐ Color 3

■ Color 4

☐ Color 5

☐ Color 6

■ Color 7

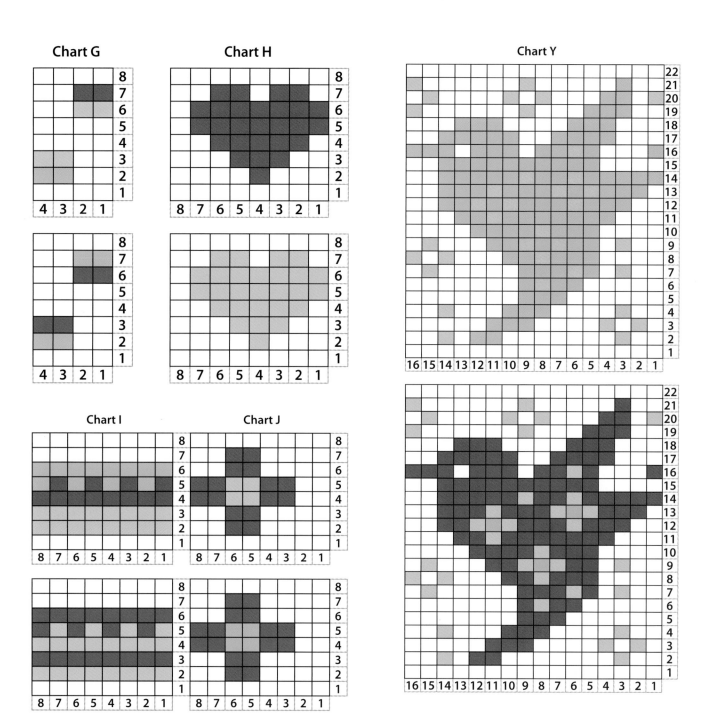

Chart K

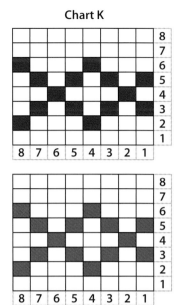

Chart L

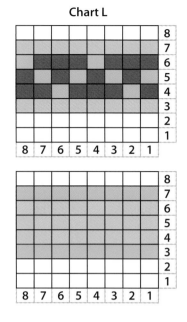

Chart M

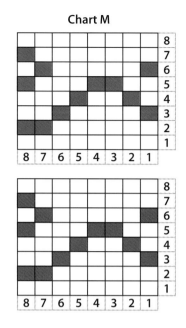

Chart N

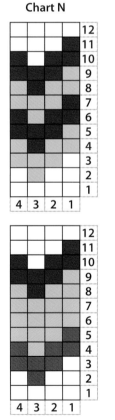

Chart O

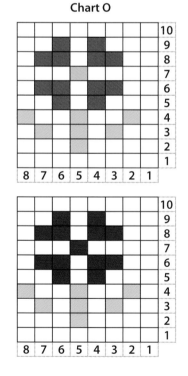

Chart P

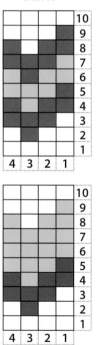

☐ Main Color

■ Color 2

▨ Color 3

■ Color 4

▨ Color 5

☐ Color 6

■ Color 7

Kitulo

95

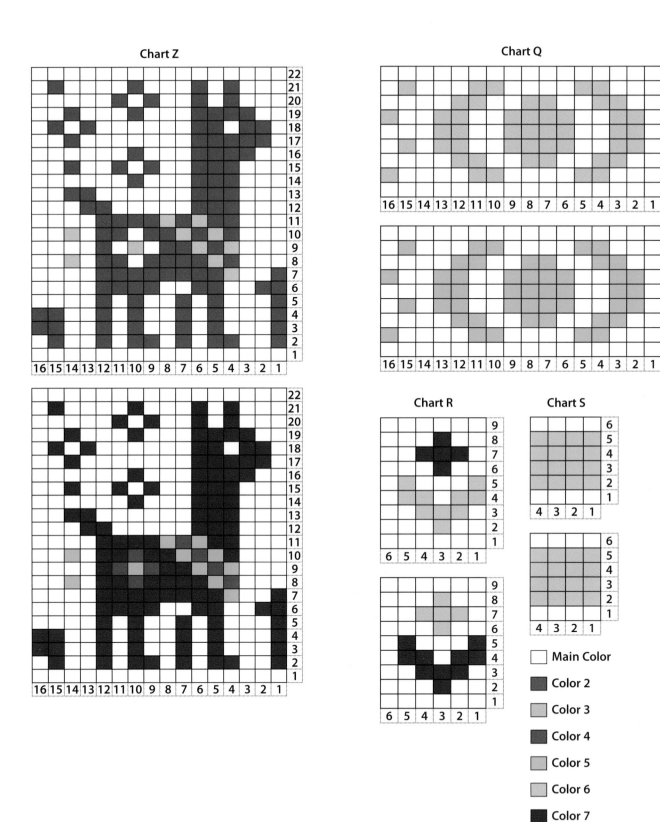

Chart Z

Chart Q

Chart R

Chart S

Main Color

Color 2

Color 3

Color 4

Color 5

Color 6

Color 7

Knit Wild

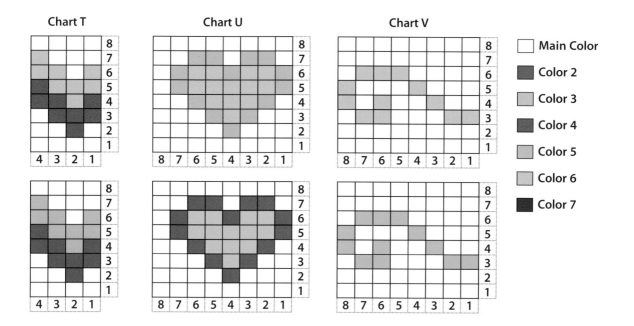

Chart T   Chart U   Chart V

Main Color

Color 2

Color 3

Color 4

Color 5

Color 6

Color 7

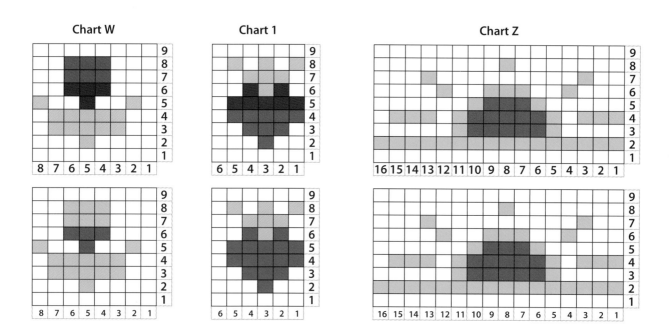

Chart W   Chart 1   Chart Z

Kitulo
KELBOURNE WOOLENS Scout +
ÍSTEX Léttlopi

C1: Scout 305 Moss Heather
C2: Scout 805 Burnt Orange Heather
C3: Léttlopi 1418 Straw
C4: Scout 278 Oatmeal Heather

Akilak

Akilak is inspired by a captivating Greenlandic children's story about the journey
of a little girl who travels through the wilderness from one village to another to
find medicine for her ailing grandma. Along the way, she befriends wild animals,
who join her in navigating the snowy landscapes.
Akilak embodies the profound bond between humans, animals, and nature.
This design is a symbol of friendship and harmony.

Akilak

Starting with a ribbed hem, the body and sleeves are worked bottom up in the round and knit separately. A steek is added to the body for later sleeve attachment. The neck is knitted by picking up stitches from the body. The arms are knitted separately and sewn into the body afterwards.

Sizes
(2XS, XS, S) (M, L, XL) (2XL, 3XL, 4XL)

Recommended ease: 4 in (10 cm) positive ease

Measurements
Chest circumference:
(35, 36.5, 39.4) (42.1, 44.5, 47.3) (50, 52.4, 55.1) in/
(80, 88, 96) (104, 112, 120) (128, 136, 144) cm

Arm circumference:
(15.7, 15.7, 15.7) (18.1, 18.1, 20.1) (22.4, 22.4, 22.4) in/
(40, 40, 40) (46, 46, 51) (57, 57, 57) cm

Yarn
Istex Plötulopi (2 strands held together); pencil roving;
100% new Icelandic wool; 328.1 yd (300 m), 3.5 oz (100 g) per disk

C1: 1425 Sunset Rose: (5, 5, 6) (6, 6, 6) (7, 7, 7) disks
C2: 2026 Amethyst: (1, 1, 1) (2, 2, 2) (2, 2, 2) disks
C3: 1424 Golden Yellow: (1, 1, 1) (2, 2, 2) (2, 2, 2) disks
C4: 2025 Gulf Stream: (1, 1, 1) (1, 1, 1) (1, 1, 1) disks

Needles
Double-pointed needles: US 7 and US 10 (4.5 mm and 6 mm)
(unless the magic loop technique is used)
Circular needles, 16 in (40 cm): US 7 and US 10 (4.5 mm and 6 mm)
Circular needles, 32 in (80 cm): US 7 and US 10 (4.5 mm and 6 mm)

Gauge
14 stitches and 20 rows = 4 in (10 cm) on US 10
needles in stockinette stitch

Body

Cast on (112, 120, 136) (144, 152, 168) (176, 192, 200) stitches with C2 using size US 7 (4.5 mm) needle. Place a stitch marker to mark the beginning of the round and after (56, 60, 68) (72, 76, 84) (88, 96, 100) stitches to mark the front and back sides. Work "knit 1, purl 1" rib. Switch to C1 after you have knit 1 round of rib and work rib to 2.75 in (7 cm). Change to size US 10 (6 mm) needle. Continue with C1 until work measures (13.4, 13.4, 14.2) (15, 15.8, 42) (16.5, 17.3, 17.3) in/(34, 36, 36) (38, 38, 40) (40, 42, 42) cm or desired length, allowing 9.4 in (24 cm) for Chart A.

Knit following chart, starting and ending where it is marked for the selected size. Once the body measures (13.4, 13.4, 14.2) (15, 15.8, 42) (16.5, 17.3, 17.3) in/(41, 41, 41) (43, 43, 45) (45, 47, 47) cm, choose between knitting the front piece and the back piece back and forth, or adding 2 extra stitches on each side between the front and back pieces if you prefer to knit in the round and cut the opening. Continue knitting chart until complete.

Place middle (37, 37, 39) (39, 39, 39) (41, 41, 41) stitches from front piece and middle (37, 37, 39) (39, 39, 39) (41, 41, 41) stitches from back piece on a size US 7 (4.5 mm) needle. You should now have (92, 92, 92) (92, 96, 96) (100, 100, 100) stitches. The remaining stitches forming the shoulders are sewn together or Kitchener grafted at the end.

Work "knit 2, purl 2" rib for 8 in (20 cm). Bind off loosely. Set the work aside and knit sleeves.

Sleeves

Cast on (36, 36, 36) (38, 38, 38) (40, 40, 40) stitches with C2 using size US 7 (4.5 mm) needle. Place a stitch marker to mark the beginning of the round. Work "knit 1, purl 1" rib. Switch to C1 after you have knit one round of the rib and work rib to 2.75 in (7 cm).

Change to size US 10 (6 mm) needle. Continue in stockinette stitch increasing 2 stitches every 5th round (1 stitch after the first stitch of the round, and 1 stitch before the last stitch of the round) until you

have (56, 56, 56) (64, 64, 72) (72, 80, 80) stitches or until work measures (15, 15.4, 17) (18.1, 19.3, 19.3) (19.3, 20, 20) in/(31, 33, 33) (35, 35, 37) (37, 39, 39) cm or desired length, allowing 5.5 in (14 cm) for Chart B. Work Chart B. Bind off loosely. Knit the second sleeve like the first.

Finishing

Sew two tight seams by hand or with a sewing machine corresponding to the width at the top of the sleeves, and then cut up between the seams. Sew in the sleeves. Afterward, weave in all ends, block the garment, and lay it flat to dry.

Knit Wild

Chart B

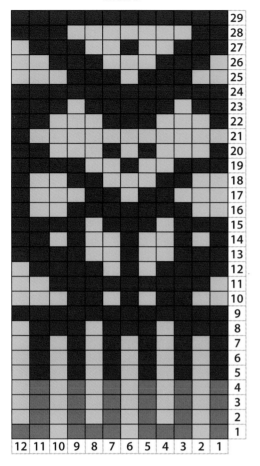

Color 1

Color 2

Color 3

Color 4

Akilak

Akilak

ÍSTEX Plötulopi held double

C1: 0005 Black Heather
C2: 1431 Artic Blue Heather
C3: 1426 Dark Amber
C4: 1427 Jasper Red

Ailo

Ailo is a name that carries a sense of wonder and adventure. It has roots
in different cultures, including the indigenous Sami people of northern
Scandinavia. In the Sami language, "Ailo" means "little son" or "little one."
The name Ailo evokes images of vast snowy landscapes, where reindeer roam freely
and the Northern Lights dance across the night sky. It represents a connection to
nature, resilience, and a spirit of exploration. The design reflects these attributes.

Ailo

Starting with a ribbed hem, the body and sleeves are worked bottom up in the round and knit separately. A steek is added to the body for later sleeve attachment. The neck is knitted by picking up stitches from the body. The arms are knitted separately and sewn into the body afterwards.

Sizes
(2XS, XS, S) (M, L, XL) (2XL, 3XL, 4XL)

Measurements
Chest circumference:
(31.5, 36, 40.6) (42.8, 43.8, 49.6) (54, 58.6, 63) in/
(80, 92, 103) (109, 115, 125) (137, 149, 160) cm

Arm circumference:
(18, 18, 18) (20.2, 20.2, 20.2) (22.5, 22.5, 25.4) in/
(46, 46, 46) (51, 51, 51) (57, 57, 65) cm

Yarn
Brooklyn Tweed Quarry; bulky weight;
100% American Targhee-Columbia wool; 200 yd (183 m),
3.5 oz (100 g) per skein

Brooklyn Tweed Shelter; worsted weight;
100% American Targhee-Columbia wool; 140 yd (128 m),
1.8 oz (50 g) per skein

C1: Quarry – Cast Iron: (5, 5, 6) (6, 6, 6) (7, 7, 7) skeins
C2: Shelter – Bale: (2, 2, 2) (3, 3, 3) (4, 4, 4) skeins
C3: Shelter – Fireball: (2, 2, 2) (3, 3, 3) (4, 4, 4) skeins
C4: Shelter – Klimt: (1, 2, 2) (2, 2, 2) (2, 3, 3) skeins
C5: Shelter – Fossil: (1, 2, 2) (2, 2, 2) (2, 3, 3) skeins

Needles
Double-pointed needles: US 7 and US 10 (4.5 mm and 6 mm)
(unless the magic loop technique is used)
Circular needles, 16 in (40 cm): US 7 and US 10 (4.5 mm and 6 mm)
Circular needles, 32 in (80 cm): US 7 and US 10 (4.5 mm and 6 mm)

Gauge
14 stitches and 20 rows = 4 in (10 cm) on US 10 needle in stockinette stitch

Other
1 or 2 Buttons

Body

Cast on (112, 128, 144) (152, 160, 176) (192, 208, 224) stitches with C1 using size US 7 (4.5 mm) circular needle. Place a stitch marker to mark the beginning of the round and after (56, 64, 72) (76, 80, 88) (96, 104, 112) stitches to mark the front and back side.

Work "knit 1, purl 1" rib for 2.75 in (7 cm). Change to size US 10 (6 mm) needle. Continue with C1 until work measures (15, 15.8, 15.8) (16.5, 16.5, 17.3) (17.3, 18.1, 18.1) in/(34, 36, 36) (38, 38, 40) (40, 42, 42) cm or desired length, allowing 11.4 in (29 cm) for Chart B.

Knit following Chart B until body measures (16.5, 16.4, 16.5) (16.9, 16.9, 17.7) (17.7, 18.5, 18.5) in/ (41, 41, 41) (43, 43, 45) (45, 47, 47) cm.

From here you can choose between knitting the front piece and the back piece back and forth, or adding 2 extra stitches in between the front piece and the back piece on each side if you prefer to knit in a round and cut the opening.

Continue knitting Chart B until row 41.

Bind off 5 stitches in the middle of the front of the sweater. This will be the new beginning of the round. From here on, the yoke is knit back and forth. Finish the pattern and knit 3 more rounds. Set aside the middle (36, 36, 36) (40, 40, 40) (40, 44, 44) (+5) stitches (which are not included in the pattern) from the front piece and the middle (36, 36, 36) (40, 40, 40) (40, 44, 44) stitches from the back piece. The remaining stitches forming the shoulders are sewn together or Kitchener grafted at the end.

Hood

Place 1 stitch marker in the middle of the back. Knit back and forth in stockinette stitch until the hood measures 18.8 in (35 cm) or the desired length.

In the next 12 rounds, we will shape the top back side of the hood. The decreases take place on the left and right sides of the stitch marker placed at the back of the head. Decrease 1 stitch on each side of the marker every 2nd round, a total of 6 times (12 stitches decreased).

Graft the underarm stitches and the hood to close.

Hood Button Band

Pick up stitches for the button band as follows: Pick up 3 stitches, skip the 4th st, and repeat this pattern until you reach the other end of the hood. Make sure to end up with an even number of stitches.

Knit 1 row in stockinette stitch, then work the ribbing "knit 1, purl 1"

Repeat these rows until the button band measures 1.5 in (4 cm) on all sizes. If desired, knit buttonholes* on the left side of the hood; otherwise, skip this step for a hood without buttons.

Bind off and sew the bottom of the button band by laying the ends over each other. Hide the steeked edges.

*Buttonholes: After 0.8 in (2 cm), knit 2 stitches together and then bind off 1 stitch. Binding off 1 stitch will fit well with 0.8–0.86 in (20–22 mm) buttons. Continue until Buttonband measures 1.5 in (4 cm) on all sizes. Bind off more stitches if you want larger buttons. Set the work aside and begin sleeves.

For a more detailed description in how to knit a button band see page 58.

Ailo

Sleeves

Cast on (32, 32, 32) (36, 36, 36) (40, 40, 40) stitches with C1 using size US 7 (4.5 mm) circular needle. Place a stitch marker to mark the beginning of the round.

Work "knit 1, purl 1" rib for 2.75 in (7 cm). Change to size US 10 (6 mm) needle. Continue in stockinette stitch increasing 2 stitches every 5th round (1 stitch after the first stitch of the round, and 1 stitch before the last st of the round) until you have (64, 64, 64) (64, 64, 80) (80, 80, 80) stitches or until work measures (14.2, 15, 15) (15.8, 15.8, 16.6) (16.6, 17, 17) in/(36, 38, 38) (40, 40, 42) (42, 44, 44) cm or desired length, allowing 4 in (10 cm) for Chart A.

Work pattern according to Chart A. Let increases run into the pattern.

Knit 3 more rounds in C2. Bind off loosely.

Knit the second sleeve like the first.

Finishing

Sew or Kitchener graft shoulders together.

If you choose to knit in a round: Sew two tight seams by hand or with a sewing machine corresponding to the width at the top of the sleeves, and then cut up between the seams. Set in sleeves.

If you choose to knit back and forth: Set in sleeves.

Afterward, add Buttons, weave in all ends, block the garment, and lay it flat to dry.

Chart B

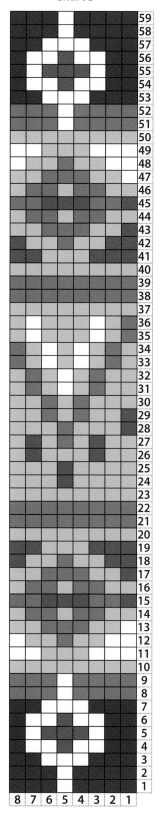

Chart A

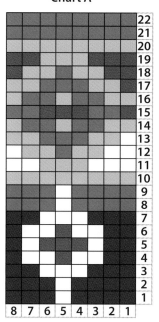

■ Color 1

□ Color 2

■ Color 3

■ Color 4

□ Color 5

Knit Wild

Ailo
BROOKLYN TWEED Quarry + Shelter
held double
C1: Quarry Barn Owl
C2: Shelter Long Johns
C3: Shelter Iceberg
C4: Shelter Klimt
C5: Quarry Fossil

Ailo
BROOKLYN TWEED Quarry +
Shelter held double
C1: Quarry Sweatshirt
C2: Shelter Long Johns
C3: Shelter Klimt
C4: Quarry Cast Iron
C5: Quarry Fossil

The Dragonfly

The dragonfly is one of the most magical beings in the animal kingdom. Dragonflies, with their vibrant colors and graceful flight, symbolize peace, happiness, hope, and personal growth—qualities we can all appreciate in our lives.

This pattern is inspired by the dragonfly's unique beauty and charm. The dragonfly's body shines brightly and exudes a glamour that's hard to resist. Inspired by its charm, I set out to "catch" the essence of this marvelous creature in this pattern. I used deep and captivating colors to mimic how they shimmer in the sunlight during their graceful flights.

The Dragonfly

K.

Starting with a ribbed hem, the body and sleeves are worked bottom up in the round and knit separately. A steek is added to the body for later sleeve attachment. The neck is knitted by picking up stitches from the body. The sleeves are knitted separately and sewn into the body afterwards.

Sizes
(2XS, XS, S) (M, L, XL) (2XL, 3XL, 4XL)

Recommended ease: 4 in (10 cm) positive ease

Measurements
Chest circumference: (88, 94, 101) (107, 113, 120) (126, 136, 148) in/
(88, 94, 101) (107, 113, 120) (126, 136, 148) cm

Arm circumference:
(15, 15, 17.4) (17.4, 19.8, 19.8) (22.1, 22.1, 24.9) in/
(38, 38, 44) (44, 50, 50) (56, 56, 63) cm

Yarn
Brooklyn Tweed Shelter; worsted weight;
100% American Targhee-Columbia wool; 140 yd (128 m),
1.8 oz (50 g) per skein

Brooklyn Tweed Tones; worsted weight;
100% American Columbia wool; 140 yd (128 m),
1.8 oz (50 g) per skein

C1: Tones – Vacay Undertone: (7, 7, 7) (8, 8, 8) (10, 10, 10) skeins
C2: Shelter – Meteorite: (2, 2, 2) (3, 3, 3) (4, 4, 4) skeins
C3: Tones – Goldfinch Undertone: (2, 2, 2) (3, 3, 3) (4, 4, 4) skeins
C4: Shelter – Embers: (1, 2, 2) (2, 2, 2) (2, 3, 3) skeins

Needles
Double-pointed needles: US 4 and US 6 (3.5 mm and 4 mm) (unless the magic loop technique is used)
Circular needles, 16 in (40 cm): US 4 and US 6 (3.5 mm and 4 mm)
Circular needles, 32 in (80 cm): US 4 and US 6 (3.5 mm and 4 mm)

Gauge
19 stitches and 26 rows = 4 in (10 cm) on US 6 needle in stockinette stitch

Body

Cast on (168, 180, 192) (204, 216, 228) (240, 264, 280) stitches with C1 using size US 4 (3.5 mm) circular needle. Place a stitch marker to mark the beginning of the round and after (84, 90, 96) (102, 108, 114) (120, 132, 140) stitches to mark front and back sides. Knit 5 rounds to achieve a rolled edge. Work "knit 2, purl 2" rib for 1.2 in (3 cm).

Change to US 6 (4 mm) size needle. Continue with C1 until work measures (15, 15.8, 15.8) (16.6, 16.6, 17.4) (17.4, 18.2, 18.2) in/(38, 40, 40) (42, 42, 44) (44, 46, 46) cm or desired length. Note: Chart C is 10.3 in (26 cm) high. Work Chart C and start and end where it is marked for the selected size.

Continue Chart C until work measures (17, 17.8, 17.8) (18.6, 18.6, 19.3) (19.3, 20.1, 20.1) in/(43, 45, 45) (47, 47, 49) (49, 51, 51) cm or desired length. From here you can choose between knitting the front piece and the back piece back and forth, or adding 2 extra stitches in between the front piece and the back piece on each side if you prefer to knit in the round and cut the opening.

Continue knitting Chart C. Set the middle (46, 46, 46) (46, 48, 48) (50, 50, 50) stitches from the front piece and the middle (46, 46, 46) (46, 48, 48) (50, 50, 50) stitches from the back piece on a US 4 (3.5 mm) needle. You should now have (92, 92, 92) (92, 96, 96) (100, 100, 100) stitches.

Work "knit 2, purl 2" rib with C1 for 1.2 in (3 cm). Knit 5 rounds to achieve a rolled edge. Loosely bind off. The remaining stitches that form the shoulders are sewn together or Kitchener grafted at the end. Set the work aside and knit sleeves.

Sleeves

Cast on (36, 36, 40) (40, 40, 44) (44, 44, 44) stitches with C1 using size US 4 (3.5 mm) circular needle. Place a stitch marker to mark the beginning of the round. Knit 5 rounds to achieve a rolled edge. Work "knit 2, purl 2" rib for 1.2 in (3cm).

Change to US 6 (4 mm) size needle. Work 1 round in C2 while increasing (14, 14, 10) (10, 10, 16) (16, 16, 16) stitches evenly over the round.

You should now have (50, 50, 50) (50, 50, 60) (60, 60, 60) stitches. Work Chart A. Continue in stockinette stitch increasing 2 stitches every 5th round (1 stitch after the first stitch of the round, and 1 stitch before the last stitch of the round) until you have (72, 72, 84) (84, 96, 96) (108, 108, 120) stitches. Let the increase stitches go into the pattern.

Continue in stockinette stitch until work measures (14.2, 15, 15) (15.8, 15.8, 16.6) (16.6, 17, 17) in/(36, 38, 38) (40, 40, 42) (42, 44, 44) cm or desired length, allowing 3.4 in (9 cm) for Chart B. Work pattern according to Chart B. Bind off loosely.

Knit the second sleeve like the first.

Finishing

Sew or Kitchener graft shoulders together.

If you choose to knit in a round: Sew two tight seams by hand or with a sewing machine corresponding to the width at the top of the sleeves, and then cut up between the seams. Set in sleeves.

If you choose to knit back and forth: Set in sleeves.

Afterward, weave in all ends, block the garment, and lay it flat to dry

The Dragonfly
ÍSTEX Léttlopi
C1: 1412 Pink
C2: 1414 Violet
C3: 1703 Mimosa
C4: 9426 Golden

Chart C

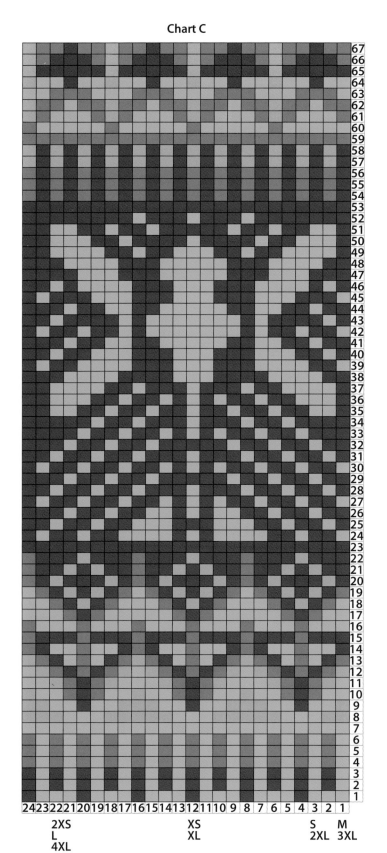

Rows 1–67, columns 24–1

Size labels:
2XS
L
4XL

XS
XL

S
2XL

M
3XL

Chart B

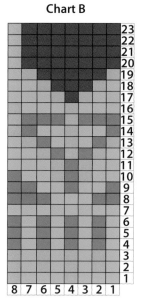

Rows 1–23, columns 8–1

Chart A

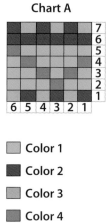

Rows 1–7, columns 6–1

- ☐ Color 1
- ■ Color 2
- ☐ Color 3
- ☐ Color 4

The Dragonfly
ÍSTEX Léttlopi
C1: 1703 Mimosa
C2: 9431 Brick
C3: 9419 Ocean Blue
C4: 9426 Golden

The Dragonfly
BERROCO Vintage
C1: 5181 Black Cherry
C2: 51180 Grapefruit
C3: 51192 Marmalade
C4: 51196 Jalapeno
C5: 5174 Rye

Forestfox

In the thick forest, a shadow wanders alone.
Red fur glints 'twixt trees galore
Above, a flight of swallows soar
As they fly deftly through the skies
Singing their sweet melodic sighs,
The fox moves lithely through the bones
Of white birch trees and ancient stones,
Weaving his way through the maze ahead
Strolling where few have dared to tread
Green leaves blot out sun and sky
While crows on branches perch to spy
So shy a beast that roams alone,
For it is alone it has always been.

Forestfox

This pattern is worked seamlessly in the round from the bottom up. First, the body and sleeves are worked up separately. Then, the body and sleeves are joined to form the yoke, which is worked in the round on a circular needle and shaped with decreases. The sweater is finished with a short folded neck.

Sizes
(2XS, XS, S) (M, L, XL) (2XL, 3XL, 4XL)

Recommended ease: 2–4 in (5–10 cm) positive ease

Measurements
Chest circumference:
(28, 31.6, 34.4) (38.3, 107, 113) (120, 133, 140) in/
(71, 80, 87) (97, 107, 113) (120, 133, 140) cm

Arm circumference:
(17.4, 17.8, 18.6) (19.7, 19.7, 19.7) (19.7, 20.5, 20.5) in/
(44, 45, 47) (50, 50, 50) (50, 52, 52) cm

Yarn
Ístex Léttlopi; worsted weight; 100% new Icelandic wool; 109 yd (99.5 m),
1.8 oz (50 g) per skein

C1: 0867 Chocolate: (8, 9, 9) (9, 10, 10) (10, 11, 11) skeins
C2: 1404 Glacier Blue: (2, 3, 3) (3, 3, 3) (4, 4, 4) skeins
C3: 1704 Apricot: (1, 1, 1) (1, 1, 2) (2, 2, 2) skeins
C4: 1416 Moor: (1, 1, 1) (1, 1, 1) 1, 1, 1) skein
C5: 0051 White: (1, 1, 1) (1, 1, 2) (2, 2, 2) skeins
C6: 1417 Frostbite: (1, 1, 1) (1, 1, 1) (1, 1, 1) skeins
C7: 9421 Celery Green: (1, 1, 1) (1, 1, 1) (1, 1, 1) skeins
C8: 1407 Pine Green: (1, 1, 1) (1, 1, 1) (1, 1, 1) skeins
C9: 9427 Rust: (1, 1, 1) (1, 1, 1) (1, 1, 1) skeins

Needles
Double-pointed needles: US 4 and US 7 (3.5 mm and 4.5 mm) (unless the magic loop technique is used)
Circular needles, 16 in (40 cm): US 4 and US 7 (3.5 mm and 4.5 mm)
Circular needles, 32 in (80 cm): US 4 and US 7 (3.5 mm and 4.5 mm)

Gauge
18 stitches and 26 rows = 4 in (10 cm) on US 7 needle in stockinette stitch

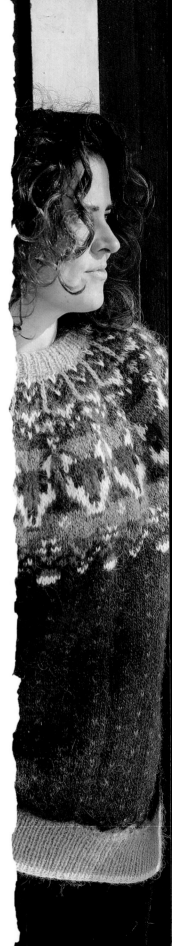

Body

Cast on (126, 144, 156) (174, 192, 204) (216, 240, 252) stitches with C5 using size US 4 (3.5 mm) needle. Place a stitch marker to mark the beginning of the round and after (63, 72, 78) (87, 96, 102) (108, 120, 126) stitches to mark front and back sides. Work 2 rounds of "knit 1, purl 1" rib and change to C3. Work "knit 1, purl 1" rib for 3 in (7.5 cm). Change to size US 7 (4.5 mm) needle. Knit 1 round. Work Chart A.

Continue in stockinette stitch while working Chart B until work measures (16.6, 16.6, 16.6) (17.4, 18.2, 19) (19, 19, 19.8) in/(42, 42, 42) (44, 46, 48) (48, 48, 50) cm or desired length.

Place the first (3, 5, 6) (6, 7, 7) (7, 8, 8) and the last (4, 5, 6) (7, 7, 8) (7, 8, 9) stitches on a stitch holder or waste yarn for underarm, a total of (7, 10, 12) (13, 14, 15) (14, 16, 17) stitches. The stitches for the other armhole will be put on holder when you start the yoke. Set the work aside and knit the sleeves.

Sleeves

Cast on (36, 36, 36) (42, 42, 48) (48, 48, 48) stitches with C5 using size US 4 (3.5 mm) needle. Place a stitch marker to mark the beginning of the round. Work 2 rounds of "knit 1, purl 1" rib and change to C3. Work "knit 1, purl 1" rib for 3 in (7.5 cm). Change to size US 7 (4.5 mm) needle. Knit 1 round. Work Chart A. Continue in stockinette stitch while working increases of 2 stitches every 5th round (1 stitch after the first stitch of the round, and 1 stitch before the last st of the round) until you have (55, 60, 66) (67, 68, 72) (72, 72, 76) stitches.

Continue with Chart B until work measures (17.8, 18.2, 18.2) (19, 20.1, 20.5) (20.5, 20.5, 22.1) in/(45, 46, 46) (48, 51, 52) (52, 52, 56) cm or desired length. Place the first (3, 5, 6) (6, 7, 7) (7, 8, 8) and the last (4, 5, 6) (7, 7, 8) (7, 8, 9) stitches on a stitch holder or waste yarn for underarm, a total of (7, 10, 12) (13, 14, 15) (14, 16, 17) stitches.

Knit the second sleeve like the first.

(Note: You will not complete Chart B under the sleeves in sizes 2XS, M, L, and 4XL.)

Yoke

Join body and sleeves on size US 7 (4.5 mm) circular needle. Place a stitch marker to mark the beginning of the round at the first join. Knit over first sleeve. Knit over front side. Transfer next (7, 10, 12) (13, 14, 15) (14, 16, 17) stitches onto stitch holder or waste yarn for underarm. Knit over the other sleeve and back side. You should now have (208, 224, 240) (256, 272, 288) (304, 320, 336) stitches.

Work pattern according to Chart C and decrease as directed. Change to shorter needle if necessary. After completing chart (78, 84, 90) (96, 102, 108) (114, 120, 126) stitches remain on needles.

Neck

Change to US 4 (3.5 mm) circular needle. Work 1 round straight with C2 while at the same time decreasing (10, 14, 18) (22, 26, 30) (34, 38, 44) stitches evenly over the round. You should now have (68, 70, 72) (74, 76, 78) (80, 82, 82) stitches.

Work "knit 1, purl 1" rib for 3.2 in (8 cm). Loosely bind off. Fold Neck.

Chart A

						10
						9
						8
						7
						6
						5
						4
						3
						2
						1
6	5	4	3	2	1	

Chart B

												6
												5
												4
												3
												2
												1
12	11	10	9	8	7	6	5	4	3	2	1	

■ Color 1

■ Color 2

■ Color 3

■ Color 4

□ Color 5

■ Color 6

■ Color 7

■ Color 8

■ Color 9

\ Decrease left leaning

/ Decrease right leaning

Chart C

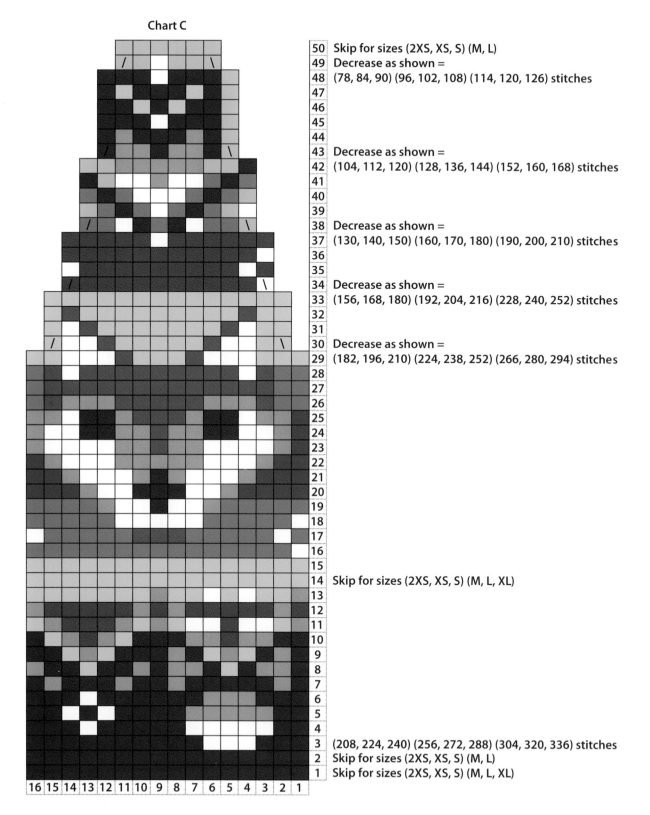

50 | Skip for sizes (2XS, XS, S) (M, L)
49 | Decrease as shown =
48 | (78, 84, 90) (96, 102, 108) (114, 120, 126) stitches
47 |
46 |
45 |
44 |
43 | Decrease as shown =
42 | (104, 112, 120) (128, 136, 144) (152, 160, 168) stitches
41 |
40 |
39 |
38 | Decrease as shown =
37 | (130, 140, 150) (160, 170, 180) (190, 200, 210) stitches
36 |
35 |
34 | Decrease as shown =
33 | (156, 168, 180) (192, 204, 216) (228, 240, 252) stitches
32 |
31 |
30 | Decrease as shown =
29 | (182, 196, 210) (224, 238, 252) (266, 280, 294) stitches
28 |
27 |
26 |
25 |
24 |
23 |
22 |
21 |
20 |
19 |
18 |
17 |
16 |
15 |
14 | Skip for sizes (2XS, XS, S) (M, L, XL)
13 |
12 |
11 |
10 |
9 |
8 |
7 |
6 |
5 |
4 |
3 | (208, 224, 240) (256, 272, 288) (304, 320, 336) stitches
2 | Skip for sizes (2XS, XS, S) (M, L)
1 | Skip for sizes (2XS, XS, S) (M, L, XL)

16 15 14 13 12 11 10 9 8 7 6 5 4 3 2 1

Refer to chart key on page 136

Forestfox
ÍSTEX Léttlopi
C1: 1703 Mimosa
C2: 1404 Glacier Blue
C3: 1704 Apricot
C4: 1416 Moor
C5: 0051 White
C6: 1700 Air Blue
C7: 9418 Stone Blue
C8: 9420 Navy Blue
C9: 19427 Rust

Sköll og Hati

Sköll is the name of the wolf
Who follows the shining priest
Into the desolate forest,
And the other is Hati,
Hróvitnir's son,
Who chases the bright bride of the sky

Sköll og Hati, unknown poet

Sköll og Hati

The body and sleeves are worked from the bottom up. The sleeves are knitted separately and sewn in afterward. Two versions are available: a simple version with ribbed edges in colors that symbolize the sun and moon, and a colorful version with a rolled ribbing. Additionally, there are two options available for knitting the chart: long or short, depending on whether you prefer a longer garment or a regular one.

Sizes
(2XS, XS, S) (M, L, XL) (2XL, 3XL, 4XL)

Measurements
Chest circumference:
(30.6, 33.6, 36.7) (39.8, 42.8, 48.9) (52, 55.1, 61.2) in/
(77, 85, 93) (101, 109, 124) (132, 140, 155) cm

Arm circumference:
(15.3, 15.3, 17.3) (17.3, 17.3, 19.7) (19.7, 19.7, 19.7) in/
(39, 39, 44) (44, 44, 50) (50, 50, 50) cm

Yarn
Ístex Léttlopi; worsted weight; 100% new Icelandic wool; 109 yd (99.5 m), 1.8 oz (50 g) per skein

Version 1:
C1: 0054 Ash: (5, 5, 6) (6, 6, 6) (7, 7, 7) skeins
C2: 0052 Black Sheep: (5, 6, 6) (7, 7, 8) (8, 8, 9) skeins
C3: 9421 Celery Green: (1, 1, 1) (1, 1, 1) (1, 1, 1) skein
C4: 1703 Mimosa: (1, 1, 1) (1, 1, 1) (2, 2, 2) skeins

Version 2:
C1: 0051 White: (1, 1, 1) (1, 2, 2) (2, 2, 2) skeins
C2: 0086 Light Beige: (2, 2, 2) (2, 3, 3) (3, 3, 3) skeins
C3: 1420 Murky: (1, 1, 1) (1, 2, 2) (2, 2, 2) skeins
C4: 0053 Acorn: (1, 1, 1) (1, 2, 2) (2, 2, 2) skeins
C5: 9431 Rust: (1, 1, 1) (1, 2, 2) (2, 2, 2) skeins
C6: 9432 Grape: (1, 1, 1) (1, 2, 2) (2, 2, 2) skeins
C7: 1414 Violet: (1, 1, 1) (1, 2, 2) (2, 2, 2) skeins
C8: 9419 Ocean Blue: (1, 1, 1) (1, 2, 2) (2, 2, 2) skeins
C9: 1407 Pine Green (1, 1, 1) (1, 2, 2) (2, 2, 2) skeins
C10: 9421 Celery Green (1, 1, 1) (1, 2, 2) (2, 2, 2) skeins
C11: 1706 Lyme Grass: (1, 1, 1) (1, 2, 2) (2, 2, 2) skeins
C12: 9426 Golden: (1, 1, 1) (1, 2, 2) (2, 2, 2) skeins
C13: 9427 Rust: (1, 1, 1) (1, 2, 2) (2, 2, 2) skeins
C14: 0052 Black Sheep (1, 1, 1) (1, 2, 2) (2, 2, 2) skeins

Needles
Double-pointed needles: US 4 and US 7 (3.5 mm and 4.5 mm) (unless the magic loop technique is used)
Circular needles, 16 in (40 cm): US 4 and US 7 (3.5 mm and 4.5 mm)
Circular needles, 32 in (80 cm): US 4 and US 7 (3.5 mm and 4.5 mm)

Gauge
18 stitches and 26 rows = 4 in (10 cm) on US 7 needle   in stockinette stitch

Body

Cast on (140, 152, 168) (180, 196, 224) (236, 252, 280) stitches with C2 using size US 4 (3.5 mm) circular needle. Place a stitch marker to mark the beginning of the round.

Version 1: Work "knit 2, purl 2" rib for 2.75 in (7 cm).

Version 2: Knit 5 rounds to achieve a rolled edge. Work "knit 2, purl 2" rib for 1.2 in (3 cm).

Change to size US 7 (4.5 mm) needle. Work 1 round while increasing (0, 2, 0) (2, 0, 0) (2, 0, 0) stitches evenly over the round. You should now have (140, 154, 168) (182, 196, 224) (238, 252, 280) stitches. Place an additional stitch marker after (70, 77, 84) (91, 98, 112) (119, 126, 140) stitches to divide the front piece and the back piece.

Choose if you prefer to work the short or longer versions of the Charts. Work pattern according to Chart A, followed by Chart B. Chart A and B are worked alternately four times in total.

Choose between knitting the front and back pieces back and forth or adding 2 extra stitches on each side between them if you prefer to knit in the round and cut the opening. Work the pattern according to Chart C, followed by one more repeat of Charts A and B. Set the work aside and knit the sleeves.

Sleeves

Cast on (36, 36, 40) (40, 40, 44) (44, 44, 44) stitches. Place a stitch marker to mark the beginning of the round.

Version 1: Work "knit 2, purl 2" rib for 2.75 in (7 cm).

Version 2: Knit 5 rounds to achieve a rolled edge. Work "knit 2, purl 2" rib for 1.2 in (3 cm).

Change to size US 7 (4.5 mm) needle. Work 1 round while increasing (14, 14, 10) (10, 10, 16) (16, 16, 16) stitches evenly over the round. You should now have (50, 50, 50) (50, 50, 60) (60, 60, 60) stitches.

Work pattern according to Chart A, followed by Chart B. Work both charts while increasing 2 stitches every 4th round until you have (70, 70, 80) (80, 80, 90) (90, 90, 90) stitches and let the increased stitches go into the pattern. Continue knitting until Chart A

has been repeated 3 times and Chart B has been repeated 2 times. Opt for either the regular or shorter length for a more tailored fit for your arms and body. Work pattern according to Chart C. Bind off loosely. Knit the second sleeve like the first.

Choose to work a high or short neck and follow the appropriate instructions below.

High Neck (Version 1)

Place the middle (46, 46, 46) (46, 48, 48) (50, 50, 50) stitches from the front piece and the middle (46, 46, 46) (46, 48, 48) (50, 50, 50) stitches from the back piece on a US 4 (3.5 mm) needle. You should now have (92, 92, 92) (92, 96, 96) (100, 100, 100) stitches. With C1 work "knit 2, purl 2" rib for 8 in (20 cm). Bind off loosely. Fold neck.

Short Neck (Version 2)

Place the middle (46, 46, 46) (46, 48, 48) (50, 50, 50) stitches from the front piece and the middle (46, 46, 46) (46, 48, 48) (50, 50, 50) stitches from the back piece on a on a US 4 (3.5 mm) needle. You should now have (92, 92, 92) (92, 96, 96) (100, 100, 100) stitches.

With C1 work "knit 2, purl 2" rib for 1.2 in (3 cm). Knit 5 rounds to achieve a rolled edge. Loosely bind off.

Finishing

Sew or Kitchener graft shoulders together.

If you choose to knit in a round: Sew two tight seams by hand or with a sewing machine corresponding to the width at the top of the sleeves, and then cut up between the seams. Set in sleeves.

If you choose to knit back and forth: Set in sleeves.

Afterward, weave in all ends, block the garment, and lay it flat to dry.

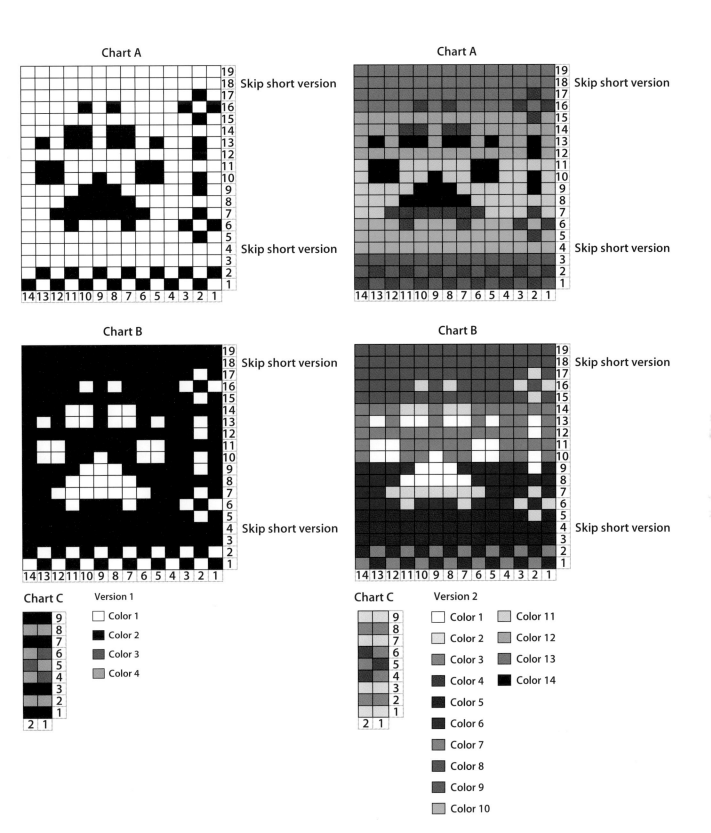

Sköll og Hati
ÍSTEX Léttlopi
C1: 1702 Milkyway
C2: 1412 Pink
C3: 9418 Stone Blue
C4: 0051 White

Honovi
BROOKLYN TWEED Tones + Ístex Léttlopi +
REVOLUTION WOOL COMPANY Harvest Yarn
C1: Tones Melba Overtone
C2: Harvest Golden Rod Yellow
C3: Léttlopi 1700 Air Blue
C4: Léttlopi 1402 Heaven Blue
C5: Léttlopi 0867 Chocolate

Honovi

Honovi, a creation that took shape in the year 2020, holds a special place in my heart as it marked my discovery of Latvian braids. Inspired by the Latvian braid's ability to infuse garments with exquisite detail, I wanted to ensure that the remaining elements of the design remained elegantly simple, allowing the braid to shine and command attention without becoming overshadowed. The result of this creative pursuit became Honovi, a garment where the mesmerizing Latvian braid takes center stage, weaving its intricate patterns with grace and finesse.

Honovi

This pattern is worked seamlessly in the round from the bottom up. The body and sleeves are worked separately. Then, they are joined to form the yoke, which is shaped with decreases to achieve a raglan fit. The sweater is finished with your choice of a turtleneck, high neck, or hood.

Sizes
(2XS, XS, S) (M, L, XL) (2XL, 3XL, 4XL)

Recommended ease: 2 in (5 cm) positive ease
(this sweater is meant to be close fitting)

Measurements
Chest circumference:
(28, 31.6, 34.4) (38.3, 107, 113) (120, 133, 140) in/
(71, 80, 87) (97, 107, 113) (120, 133, 140) cm

Arm circumference:
(17.4, 17.8, 18.6) (19.7, 19.7, 19.7) (19.7, 20.5, 20.5) in/
(44, 45, 47) (50, 50, 50) (50, 52, 52) cm

Yarn
Ístex Léttlopi; worsted weight; 100% new Icelandic wool;
109 yd (99.5 m), 1.8 oz (50 g) per skein

C1: 0085 Oatmeal: (7, 7, 8) (8, 8, 8) (10, 10, 11) skeins
C2: 1704 Apricot: (7, 7, 8) (8, 8, 8) (10, 10, 11) skeins
C3: 0053 Acorn: (1, 1, 1) (1, 1, 1) (2, 2, 2) skeins
C4: 9427 Rust: (1, 1, 1) (1, 1, 1) (2, 2, 2) skeins
C5: 1418 Light Beige (only used in Latvian braid): 1 skein all sizes

Needles
Double-pointed needles: US 4 and US 7 (3.5 mm and 4.5 mm)
(unless the magic loop technique is used)
Circular needles, 16 in (40 cm): US 4 and US 7 (3.5 mm and 4.5 mm)
Circular needles, 32 in (80 cm): US 4 and US 7 (3.5 mm and 4.5 mm)

Gauge
18 stitches and 26 rows = 4 in (10 cm) on US 7 needle
in stockinette stitch

Body

Cast on (140, 150, 160) (180, 190, 200) (210, 220, 230) stitches with C1 using size US 4 (3.5 mm) circular needle. Place a stitch marker to mark the beginning of the round and a second marker after (70, 75, 80) (90, 95, 100) (105, 110, 115) stitches to mark the front and back sides.

Work "knit 2, purl 2" rib for 4 in (10 cm). Change to a US 7 (4.5 mm) circular needle.

Knit 1 round in C1. Knit Chart A. Continue with C1 in stockinette stitch until work measures (11, 11, 12) (12.6, 13.8, 13.8) (13.8, 13.8, 14.2) in/(28, 28, 30) (32, 35, 35) (35, 35, 36) cm or desired length, allowing 4 in (10 cm) for Chart C.

Knit Chart C.

Place the first (2, 2, 3) (4, 4, 5) (5, 5, 6) stitches of the beginning of a round and the last (3, 2, 3) (4, 3, 4) (6, 5, 6) stitches onto a stitch holder or waste yarn for underarm, a total of (5, 4, 6) (8, 7, 9) (11, 10, 12) stitches. The stitches for the other armhole will be put on holder when you start the yoke. Set the work aside and begin sleeves

Sleeves

Cast on (36, 36, 36) (36, 36, 40) (40, 40, 40) stitches with C1 using size US 4 (3.5 mm) circular needle. Place a stitch marker to mark the beginning of the round.

Work "knit 2, purl 2" rib for 4 in (10 cm). Change to a US 7 (4.5 mm) circular needle. Knit 1 round in C1 while increasing (4, 4, 4) (4, 4, 10) (10, 10, 10) stitches evenly over the round. You should now have (40, 40, 40) (40, 40, 50) (50, 50, 50) stitches.

Knit Chart B.

Continue in stockinette stitch with C2 while increasing 2 stitches (1 stitch after the first stitch on round and 1 stitch before the last stitch on round). Repeat increases every 5th round. Knit (2.8, 2.8, 3.2) (3.2, 3.5, 3.5) (3.9, 3.9, 3.9) in/(7, 7, 8) (8, 9, 9) (10, 10, 10) cm (while still increasing) or desired length, allowing 4 in (10 cm) for Chart C. Knit Chart C. Work Chart C while still increasing up to (48, 48, 54) (54, 54, 60) (66, 66, 72) stitches.

Place the first (2, 2, 3) (4, 4, 5) (5, 5, 6) stitches of the beginning of a round and the last (3, 2, 3) (4, 3, 4) (6, 5, 6) stitches onto a st holder or waste yarn for underarm, a total (5, 4, 6) (8, 7, 9) (11, 10, 12) stitches.

Knit the second sleeve like the first.

Raglan

Join body and sleeves with C2 on size US 7 (4.5 mm) circular needle. Place a stitch marker between every joining piece. Place an additional stitch marker at the first join to mark the start of the round = 4 (+1) markers placed. Knit over first sleeve. Knit the front. Knit over the other sleeve and back. You should now have (208, 224, 240) (256, 272, 288) (304, 320, 336) stitches. From here, we will shape the raglan.

Raglan Decrease: On each side of the marked stitches, decrease 1 stitch to the left and 1 stitch to the right (2 stitches per join), a total of 8 stitches decreased per round every 2nd round. On the right side of marker, decrease by knitting 2 stitches together through the back loops of the stitches. On the left side of the marker, decrease by knitting 2 stitches together. Change to a shorter circular needle if necessary.

Repeat decrease every other round until you have (78, 84, 90) (96, 102, 108) (114, 120, 126) stitches left.

Choose whether you will work a turtleneck, high neck, or hood and follow the appropriate instructions that follow.

High Neck

Knit 1 round and decrease to (92, 92, 92) (92, 96, 96) (100, 100, 100) stitches. Change to size US 4 (3.5 mm) circular needle. Work "knit 2, purl 2" rib for 3 in (7.5 cm). Bind off loosely. Fold neck.

Turtleneck

Knit 1 round and decrease to (92, 92, 92) (92, 96, 96) (100, 100, 100) stitches. Change to size US 4 (3.5 mm) circular needle. Work "knit 2, purl 2" rib for 8 in (20 cm). Bind off loosely.

Hood

Knit 2 rounds. Knit 1 more round and increase by 6 stitches on all sizes. Place 1 stitch marker in the middle of the front marking the new beginning of the round. (Slip stitches in between without knitting them to get to the point. This marks also where the chart should be placed.) Knit 1 round and cast on 7 stitches at the end of the round—those are the steek stitches which will be cut later on. If you prefer, knit back and forth and ignore the steeking options.

Work Charts in the following order: X-Z-Y. Both arrows will need to face each other in the front while the Chart Pattern Z is repeated after Chart X has been knit and before starting Chart Y. For a simplified look, knit Chart Z all the way. Keep on knitting the hood for 11 in (28 cm) or the desired length.
In the next 12 rounds, shape the top backside of the hood. The decreases take place on the left and right sides from the stitch marker placed at the back of the head. Decrease 1 stitch on each side of the marker every 2nd round for a total of 6 times (12 stitches decreased). Cut the steek. Use the Kitchener stitch to close the top of the hood.

Finishing

Use Kitchener stitch to graft the underarms. Fix loose ends. Voila!

Chart A

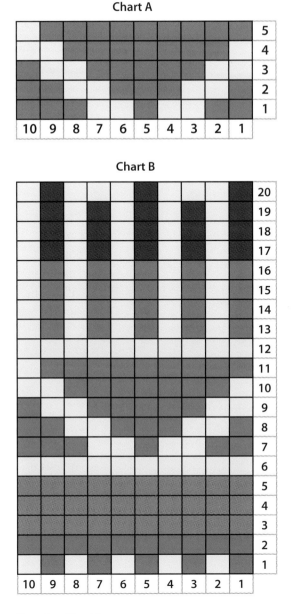

Chart B

Chart C

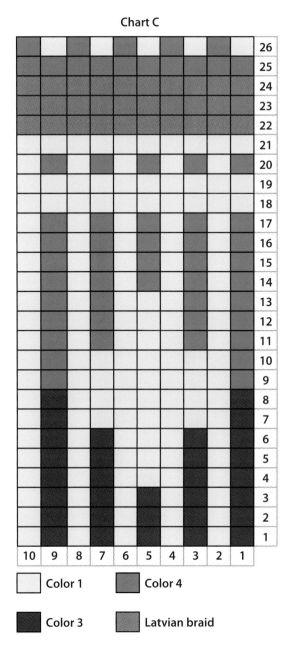

Color 1 □   Color 4 ▨

Color 3 ■   Latvian braid ▨

Latvian Braid

To knit the Latvian braid along the hood, pick up stitches as follows: Pick up 3 stitches, skip the 4th st, and repeat until you reach the other end of the hood. Knit the Latvian braid as follows:

Round 1: Knit 1 stitch with C3, followed by 1 stitch with C5, repeating this pattern until you reach the end of the round.

Round 2: With both C3 and C5 in the front, purl 1 stitch with C3, then bring C5 under C3 and purl 1 stitch with C5. Next, bring C3 under C5, and continue this pattern until the end of the round.

Round 3: Purl 1 stitch with C3, then bring C5 over C3 and purl 1 stitch with C3 again. Repeat this sequence, bringing C5 over C3 each time, until you complete the round.

Bind off using Tubular Bind-off by first alternately knitting 1 and slipping 1 stitch, then grafting all stitches together using a tapestry needle, resulting in a stretchy, seamless edge.

Honovi   157

Chart X

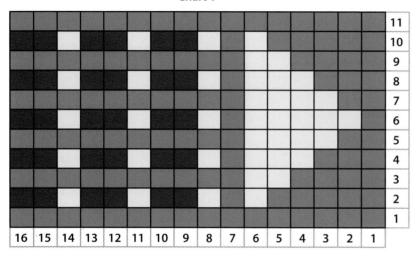

Chart Y

Latvian Braid

Chart Z

☐	Color 1
■	Color 3
▨	Color 4
▨	Latvian braid

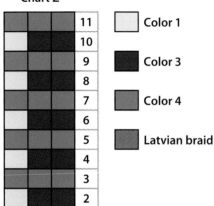

To knit the Latvian braid along the hood, pick up stitches as follows: Pick up 3 stitches, skip the 4th st, and repeat until you reach the other end of the hood. Knit the Latvian braid as follows:

Round 1: Knit 1 stitch with C3, followed by 1 stitch with C5, repeating this pattern until you reach the end of the round.

Round 2: With both C3 and C5 in the front, purl 1 stitch with C3, then bring C5 under C3 and purl 1 stitch with C5. Next, bring C3 under C5, and continue this pattern until the end of the round.

Round 3: Purl 1 stitch with C3, then bring C5 over C3 and purl 1 stitch with C3 again. Repeat this sequence, bringing C5 over C3 each time, until you complete the round.

Bind off using Tubular Bind-off by first alternately knitting 1 and slipping 1 stitch, then grafting all stitches together using a tapestry needle, resulting in a stretchy, seamless edge.

Knit Wild

Eldlauv

Eldlauv is a creation that emerged from a series of challenging days and a sense of creative stagnation. It symbolizes the triumph over moments of uncertainty and the return of inspiration in the most unexpected places. During a stroll through my untamed garden, my eyes fell upon bushes of red currants. Their vibrant presence breathed new life into me. Eldlauv stands for the transformative power of nature's beauty and the resilience of creativity. It encapsulates the journey from feeling uninspired and idea-less to rediscovering the joy of creativity through the simplest yet captivating encounters.

Eldlauv

This pattern is worked seamlessly in the round from the bottom up. First, the body and sleeves are worked separately. Then, they are joined to form the yoke, which is shaped with decreases and worked in the round on a circular needle. The sweater is finished with a rolled neck.

Sizes
(2XS, XS, S) (M, L, XL) (2XL, 3XL, 4XL)

Recommended ease: 2 in (5 cm) positive ease

Measurements
Chest circumference: (28.8, 31.6, 34) (39.5, 43.3, 44.6) (47.4, 50.2, 52.2) in/ (73, 80, 86) (100, 107, 113) (120, 127, 133) cm

Arm circumference: (19, 19, 21.3) (21.3, 21.3, 23.7) (26, 26, 28) in/ (26, 26, 30) (30, 30, 33) (37, 37, 40) cm

Yarn
Ístex Léttlopi; worsted weight; 100% new Icelandic wool; 109 yd (99.5 m), 1.8 oz (50 g) per skein

C1: 1407 Pine Green: (8, 8, 10) (10, 10, 12) (12, 14, 14) skeins
C2: 9431 Brick: (1, 1, 1) (1, 1, 1) (1, 1, 1) skeins
C3: 1703 Mimosa: (1, 1, 1) (1, 1, 1) (1, 1, 1) skeins
C4: 1704 Apricot: (1, 1, 1) (1, 1, 1) (1, 1, 1) skeins

Needles
Double-pointed needles: US 4 and US 7 (3.5 mm and 4.5 mm) (unless the magic loop technique is used)
Circular needles, 16 in (40 cm): US 4 and US 7 (3.5 mm and 4.5 mm)
Circular needles, 32 in (80 cm): US 4 and US 7 (3.5 mm and 4.5 mm)

Gauge
19 stitches and 26 rows = 4 in (10 cm) on US 7 needle in stockinette stitch

Body

Cast on (132, 144, 156) (180, 192, 204) (216, 228, 240) stitches with C1 using US 4 (3.5 mm) circular needle. Place a stitch marker to mark the beginning of the round and a second marker after (66, 72, 78) (90, 96, 102) (108, 114, 120) stitches to mark the front and back pieces.

Work "knit 1, purl 1" rib for 2.75 in (7 cm).
Change to US 7 (4.5 mm) size needle. Continue in stockinette stitch until work measures (18, 18.5, 19.25) (19.5, 19.75, 20) (20.5, 20.75, 21.25) in/(46, 47, 48) (49, 50, 51) (52, 53, 54) cm or desired length.
Place the first (2, 2, 3) (4, 4, 5) (5, 5, 6) stitches and the last (3, 2, 3) (4, 3, 4) (6, 5, 6) stitches of the round on a sleeve holder for armholes, a total of (5, 4, 6) (8, 7, 9) (11, 10, 12) stitches. The stitches for the second armhole will be put on holder when you start on the yoke. Set the work aside and knit sleeves.

Sleeves

Cast on (36, 36, 36) (36, 36, 40) (40, 40, 40) stitches with C1 using US 4 (3.5 mm) circular needle. Place a stitch marker to mark the beginning of the round.
Work "knit 1, purl 1" rib for 2.75 in (7 cm).
Change to US 7 (4.5 mm) size needle. Increase (0, 0, 0) (0, 0, 2) (2, 2, 2) stitches evenly over round = (36, 36, 36) (36, 36, 42) (42, 42, 42) stitches.
Continue in stockinette stitch increasing 2 stitches every 5th round (1 stitch after the first stitch of the round, and 1 stitch before the last st of the round) until you have (48, 48, 54) (54, 54, 60) (66, 66, 72) stitches.
Continue in stockinette stitch until work measures (18.25, 18.25, 18.5) (18.75, 19.25, 19.75) (19.75, 20, 20) in/(46, 46, 47) (48, 49, 50) (50, 51, 51) cm. Place the first (2, 2, 3) (4, 4, 5) (5, 5, 6) stitches and last (3, 2, 3) (4, 3, 4) (6, 5, 6) stitches of the round on a stitch holder for armholes, a total of (5, 4, 6) (8, 7, 9) (11, 10, 12) stitches.
Knit the second sleeve like the first.

Yoke

Join body and sleeves on size US 7 (4.5 mm) circular needle. Place a stitch marker to mark the beginning of the round at the first join. Knit over first sleeve. Knit over front side. Transfer next (5, 4, 6) (8, 7, 9) (11, 10, 12) stitches onto a stitch holder or waste yarn for underarm. Knit over the other sleeve and back side. You should now have (208, 224, 240) (256, 272, 288) (304, 320, 336) stitches.
Knit (14, 14, 16) (18, 22, 24) (26, 28, 32) rounds with C1.
Knit 1 round in stockinette stitch while at the same time decreasing (32, 32, 32) (32, 32, 32) (32, 32, 32) stitches evenly. You should now have (176, 192, 208) (224, 240, 256) (272, 288, 304) stitches.
Work pattern according to Chart and decrease as directed. Change to shorter needle if necessary. After completing chart (78, 84, 90) (96, 102, 108) (114, 120, 126) stitches remain on needles.

Neck

Change to US 4 (3.5 mm) circular needle. With C1 work 1 round even while at the same time decreasing (12, 12, 12) (16, 20, 20) (20, 26, 30) stitches evenly over the round. You should now have (66, 72, 78) (80, 82, 88) (94, 94, 96) stitches.
Work 5 rounds stockinette stitch in C1 to achieve rolled edge. Loosely bind off.

Finishing

Graft the underarm stitches to close, then weave in all ends. Block the garment and lay it flat to dry.

Chart

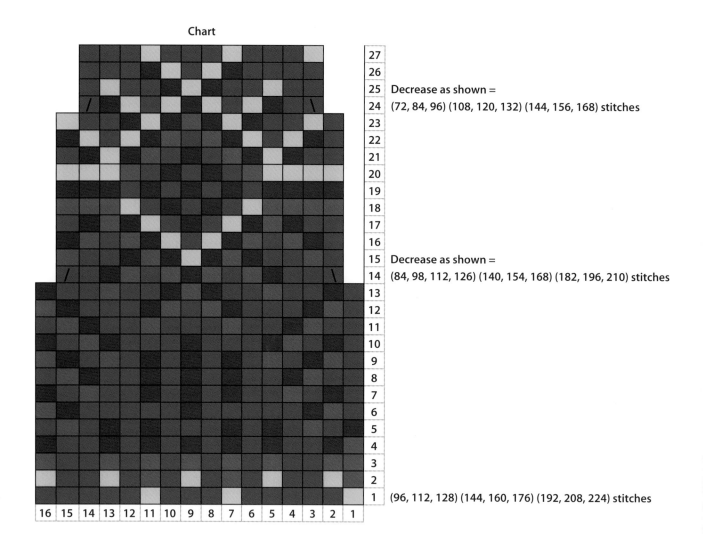

27	
26	
25	Decrease as shown =
24	(72, 84, 96) (108, 120, 132) (144, 156, 168) stitches
23	
22	
21	
20	
19	
18	
17	
16	
15	Decrease as shown =
14	(84, 98, 112, 126) (140, 154, 168) (182, 196, 210) stitches
13	
12	
11	
10	
9	
8	
7	
6	
5	
4	
3	
2	
1	(96, 112, 128) (144, 160, 176) (192, 208, 224) stitches

| 16 | 15 | 14 | 13 | 12 | 11 | 10 | 9 | 8 | 7 | 6 | 5 | 4 | 3 | 2 | 1 |

■ Color 1	\	Decrease left leaning
■ Color 2	/	Decrease right leaning
■ Color 3		
■ Color 4		

Eldlaur
ÍSTEX LÉttlopi
C1: 0053 Acorn
C2: 0057 Grey
C3: 0056 Light Grey
C4: 1418 Straw

Koyuki

"Koyuki," a name that translates to "snowflake" in Japanese, holds a special place in my heart. A dog named Koyuki was my cherished companion, a beloved Japanese Shiba Inu. Koyuki's journey began in Nagoya, Japan, and together we went on countless adventures, traversing countries such as Germany, Denmark, the Netherlands, Norway, and the United States. Whenever waves of nostalgia wash over me, I find comfort in wearing this cherished sweater. Through its warmth,
I can feel Koyuki's presence, as if she is still by my side.
This design reminds us of the profound impact our four-legged companions have on our lives and the precious memories we hold dear. It is a symbol of the enduring bond we share with our beloved pets, I hope this sweater will also bring you solace and warmth. It is a tribute to the unwavering love and loyalty that Koyuki gave me.

Koyuki

This pattern is worked seamlessly in the round from the bottom up.
First, the body and sleeves are worked up separately. Then, the body
and sleeves are joined to form the yoke, which is worked in the round
on a circular needle and shaped with decreases to achieve a raglan fit.
The sweater is finished with a turtleneck or high neck.

Sizes
(2XS, XS, S) (M, L, XL) (2XL, 3XL, 4XL)

Recommended ease: 4 in (10 cm) positive ease

Measurements
Chest circumference:
(31.2, 34, 37.1) (40.3, 43.8, 47.4) (50.1, 54.1, 57.6) in/
(78, 86, 94) (102, 111, 120) (129, 137, 146) cm

Arm circumference:
(14.6, 15.4, 15.8) (16.2, 17, 17.4) (18.2, 18.6, 19.3) in/
(37, 39, 40) (41, 43, 44) (46, 47, 49) cm

Yarn
Brooklyn Tweed Shelter (2 strands held together); worsted weight;
100% American Targhee-Columbia wool; 140 yd (128 m), 1.8 oz (50
g) per skein

C1: Klimt: (10, 10, 11) (11, 12, 12) (13, 13, 14) skeins
C2: Old World: (1, 1, 1) (1, 1, 1) (1, 1, 1) skeins
C3: Blanket Fort: (1, 1, 1) (1, 1, 1) (1, 1, 1) skeins
C4: Camper: (1, 1, 1) (1, 1, 1) (1, 1, 1) skeins
C5: Homemade Jam: (1, 1, 1) (1, 1, 1) (1, 1, 1) skeins

Needles
Double-pointed needles: US 7 and US 10 (4.5 mm and 6 mm)
(unless the magic loop technique is used)
Circular needles, 16 in (40 cm): US 7 and US 10 (4.5 mm and 6 mm)
Circular needles, 32 in (80 cm): US 7 and US 10 (4.5 mm and 6 mm)

Gauge
14 stitches and 20 rows = 4 in (10 cm) on US 10 needle in stockinette
stitch

Note: If using Brooklyn Tweed Shelter or similar weight yarn, work
with two strands held together throughout. Be sure to check gauge.

Body

Cast on (108, 120, 132) (144, 156, 168) (180, 192, 204) stitches with C1 using size US 7 (4.5 mm) circular needle. Place a stitch marker to mark the beginning of the round and a second marker after (52, 60, 66) (72, 78, 84) (90, 96, 102) stitches to mark the front and back pieces.

Work "knit 1, purl 1" rib for 4 in (10 cm).

Change to a US 10 (6 mm) circular needle. Continue in stockinette stitch until work measures (16.5, 16.5, 16.5) (17.3, 18.1, 18.9) (18.9, 18.9, 19.7) in/(42, 42, 42) (44, 46, 48) (48, 48, 50) cm or desired length. Place the first (3, 3, 4) (4, 5, 5) (6, 6, 7) stitches of the beginning of the round and the last (2, 3, 3) (4, 4, 5) (5, 6, 6) stitches onto a stitch holder or waste yarn for underarm, a total of (5, 6, 7) (8, 9, 10) (11, 12, 13) stitches. The stitches for the second armhole will be put on holder when you start on the yoke. Set the work aside and knit sleeves.

Sleeves

Cast on (34, 34, 34) (36, 36, 38) (40, 40, 40) stitches with C2 using a US 7 (4.5 mm) circular needle. Place a stitch marker to mark the beginning of the round. Work "knit 1, purl 1" rib for 4 in (10 cm).

Change to a US 10 (6 mm) circular needle. Continue in stockinette stitch increasing 2 stitches every 5th round (1 stitch after the first stitch of the round, and 1 stitch before the last st of the round) until you have (52, 54, 56) (58, 60, 62) (64, 66, 68) stitches. Continue in stockinette stitch until work measures (18.1, 18.1, 18.5) (18.9, 19.3, 19.7) (19.7, 20.1, 20.1) in/(46, 46, 47) (48, 49, 50) (50, 51, 51) cm or desired length.

Place the first (3, 3, 4) (4, 5, 5) (6, 6, 7) stitches of the beginning of the round and the last (2, 3, 3) (4, 4, 5) (5, 6, 6) stitches onto a stitch holder or waste yarn for underarm, a total of (5, 6, 7) (8, 9, 10) (11, 12, 13) stitches.

Knit the second sleeve like the first.

Yoke

Join body and sleeves on size US 10 (6 mm) circular needle. Place a stitch marker between every joining piece. Place an additional stitch marker at the first join to mark the start of the round = 4 (+1) markers placed. Knit over first sleeve. Knit the front. Knit over the other sleeve and back. You should now have (192, 204, 216) (228, 240, 252) (264, 276, 288) stitches. Knit first (0.4, 0.4, 0.4) (0.6, 0.6, 0.8) (0.8, 1.2, 1.2) in/(1, 1, 1) (1.5, 1.5, 2) (2, 3, 3) cm in stockinette stitch.

From here, we will shape the raglan.
Raglan Decrease: On each side of the marked stitches, decrease 1 stitch to the left and 1 stitch to the right (2 stitches per join), a total of 8 stitches decreased per round every 2nd round. On the right side of marker, decrease by knitting 2 stitches together through the back loops of the stitches. On the left side of the marker, decrease by knitting 2 stitches together. Change to a shorter circular needle if necessary. Repeat decrease every other round until you have knitted (14, 15, 16) (17, 18, 19) (20, 21, 22) rounds from joining edge.

Here we will now shape the seamless seam. Bind off the work. Now we will pick up all the stitches we just bound off. Knit 1 row by knitting through the last stitches before the bind off. I recommend using 1 needle size smaller as the stitches are very tight here. Now we have created the seam. Knit Chart, centering it in the front as it will not exactly match your stitch count as you keep on with raglan decrease.

Choose whether to work a high neck or turtleneck and follow the appropriate instructions below.

High Neck

Repeat decrease every other round and knit 2 in (5 cm) more or until (64, 68, 72) (68, 72, 76) (72, 76, 80) stitches remain on needles.

Knit 1 round and decrease to (64, 64, 68) (68, 68, 68) (72, 72, 76) stitches.

Change to size US 7 (4.5 mm) circular needle. Work "knit 2, purl 2" rib for 3 in (7.5 cm). Bind off loosely.

Turtleneck

Repeat decrease every other round and knit 2 in (5 cm) more or until (64, 68, 72) (68, 72, 76) (72, 76, 80) stitches remain on needles.

Change to size US 7 (4.5 mm) circular needle. Work "knit 2, purl 2" rib for 8 in (20 cm). Bind off loosely. Fold neck.

Finishing

Graft the underarm stitches to close, then weave in all ends. Block the garment and lay it flat to dry. Finally, fold the neck.

Chart

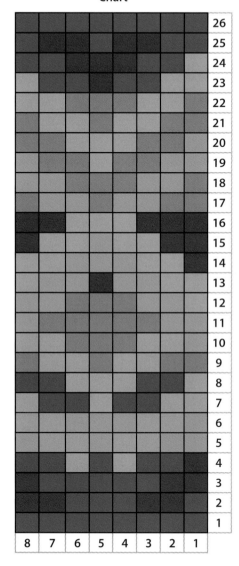

	Color 1
	Color 2
	Color 3
	Color 4
	Color 5

Koyuki
ÍSTEX Álafosslopi
C1: 9974 Light Grey Tweed
C2: 0052 Black Sheep
C3: 9971 Amber
C4: 1232 Arctic Exposure
C5: 0057 Grey

Lautarferð
The Picnic Sweater

"Lautarferð" is the Icelandic word for "picnic." This sweater is more than just a garment;
it's a companion for picnics, hikes, and cozy evenings in the garden. I envisioned a design that
exudes simplicity and authenticity, making it perfect for any occasion. Timeless and classic,
this sweater can be passed down through generations, holding tight its enduring charm.

Lautarferð
ÍSTEX Léttlopi
C1: 0056 Light Grey
C2: 0053 Acorn
C3: 0086 Light Beige
C4: 9418 Stone Blue
C5: 1402 Heaven Blue

Lautarferð

This pattern is worked seamlessly in the round from the bottom up. First, the body and sleeves are worked up separately. Then, the body and sleeves are joined to form the yoke, which is worked in the round on a circular needle and shaped with decreases. The sweater is finished with a rolled neck.

Sizes
(2XS, XS, S) (M, L, XL) (2XL, 3XL, 4XL)

Recommended ease: 4 in (10 cm) positive ease

Measurements
Chest circumference: (28, 31.6, 33.2) (38.7, 42.3, 45.4) (47.4, 49, 52.2) in/
(71, 80, 84) (98, 107, 115) (120, 124, 133) cm

Arm circumference: (17.4, 17.8, 18.6) (19.7, 19.7, 19.7) (19.7, 20.5, 20.5) in/
(44, 45, 47) (50, 50, 50) (50, 52, 52) cm

Yarn
Ístex Léttlopi; worsted weight; 100% new Icelandic wool;
109 yd (99.5 m), 1.8 oz (50 g) per skein

C1: 0054 Ash: (7, 7, 7) (8, 8, 9) (9, 10, 10) skeins
C2: 9427 Rust: (2, 2, 2) (3, 3, 3) (3, 3, 3) skeins
C3: 1404 Glacier Blue: (1, 1, 1) (1, 1, 1) (1, 1, 1) skein
C4: 1703 Mimosa: (1, 1, 1) (1, 1, 1) (2, 2, 2) skeins
C5: 9421 Celery Green: (1, 1, 1) (1, 1, 1) (1, 1, 1) skein

Needles
Double-pointed needles: US 4 and US 7 (3.5 mm and 4.5 mm) (unless the magic loop technique is used)
Circular needles, 16 in (40 cm): US 4 and US 7 (3.5 mm and 4.5 mm)
Circular needles, 32 in (80 cm): US 4 and US 7 (3.5 mm and 4.5 mm)

Gauge
18 stitches and 26 rows = 4 in (10 cm) on US 7 needle in stockinette stitch

Body

Cast on (128, 144, 160) (176, 192, 208) (216, 240, 256) stitches with C1 using a US 4 (3.5 mm) circular needle. Place a stitch marker to mark the beginning of the round and after (64, 72, 80) (88, 96, 104) (108, 120, 128) stitches to mark the front and back pieces.

Work "knit 2, purl 2" rib for 2.75 in (7 cm).

Change to size US 7 (4.5 mm) needle. Knit 1 round. Work pattern according to Chart A.

Continue in stockinette stitch using C1 until work measures (16.6, 16.6, 16.6) (17.4, 18.2, 19) (19, 19, 19.8) in/(42, 42, 42) (44, 46, 48) (48, 48, 50) cm or desired length.

Place the first (3, 5, 7) (7, 7, 7) (7, 8, 9) and the last (4, 5, 7) (7, 7, 7) (7, 8, 9) stitches on a stitch holder or waste yarn for underarm, a total of (7, 10, 14) (14, 14, 14) (14, 16, 18) stitches. The stitches for the other armhole will be placed on holder when you start the yoke. Set the work aside and knit sleeves.

Sleeves

Cast on (32, 32, 40) (40, 40, 48) (48, 48, 48) stitches with C1 using size US 4 (3.5 mm) circular needle. Place a stitch marker to mark the beginning of the round.

Work "knit 2, purl 2" rib for 2.75 in (7 cm).

Change to US 7 (4.5 mm) size needle. Knit 1 round. Work pattern according to Chart A.

Continue to knit in stockinette stitch using C1 increasing 2 stitches every 5th round until you have (54, 60, 68) (68, 68, 68) (72, 72, 76) stitches.

Continue in stockinette stitch until work measures (18.25, 18.25, 18.5) (18.75, 19.25, 19.75) (19.75, 20, 20) in/(46, 46, 47) (48, 49, 50) (50, 51, 51) cm or desired length.

Place the first (3, 5, 7) (7, 7, 7) (7, 8, 9) stitches and the last (4, 5, 7) (7, 7, 7) (7, 8, 9) stitches onto a stitch holder or waste yarn for underarm, a total of (7, 10, 14) (14, 14, 14) (14, 16, 18) stitches.

Knit the second sleeve like the first.

Yoke

Join body and sleeves on a US 7 (4.5 mm) size circular needle. Place a stitch marker to mark the beginning of the round at the first join. Knit over first sleeve. Work the front piece and transfer next (7, 10, 14) (14, 14, 14) (14, 16, 18) stitches onto a stitch holder or waste yarn for underarm. Knit over the other sleeve and back piece. You should now have (208, 224, 240) (256, 272, 288) (304, 320, 336) stitches. Work pattern according to Chart B and decrease as directed. Change to shorter needle when necessary. After completing chart (78, 84, 90) (96, 102, 108) (114, 120, 126) stitches remain on needles.

Neck

Change to size US 4 (3.5 mm) needle. Knit 1 round with C1, decreasing (6, 8, 10) (20, 20, 20) (20, 30, 30) stitches evenly over the round. You should now have (72, 76, 80) (76, 82, 88) (94, 90, 96) stitches on needles.

Knit 5 rounds to achieve a rolled edge. Bind off loosely.

Finishing

Graft underarm stitches to close. Weave in all ends. Block and lay flat to dry

Chart B

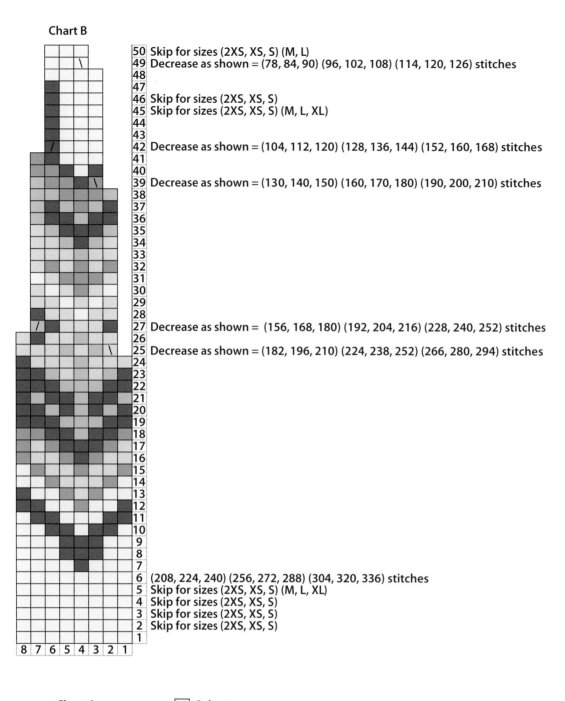

50 Skip for sizes (2XS, XS, S) (M, L)
49 Decrease as shown = (78, 84, 90) (96, 102, 108) (114, 120, 126) stitches
48
47
46 Skip for sizes (2XS, XS, S)
45 Skip for sizes (2XS, XS, S) (M, L, XL)
44
43
42 Decrease as shown = (104, 112, 120) (128, 136, 144) (152, 160, 168) stitches
41
40
39 Decrease as shown = (130, 140, 150) (160, 170, 180) (190, 200, 210) stitches
38
37
36
35
34
33
32
31
30
29
28
27 Decrease as shown = (156, 168, 180) (192, 204, 216) (228, 240, 252) stitches
26
25 Decrease as shown = (182, 196, 210) (224, 238, 252) (266, 280, 294) stitches
24
23
22
21
20
19
18
17
16
15
14
13
12
11
10
9
8
7
6 (208, 224, 240) (256, 272, 288) (304, 320, 336) stitches
5 Skip for sizes (2XS, XS, S) (M, L, XL)
4 Skip for sizes (2XS, XS, S)
3 Skip for sizes (2XS, XS, S)
2 Skip for sizes (2XS, XS, S)
1

8 7 6 5 4 3 2 1

Chart A

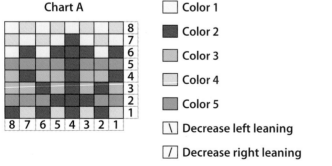

8
7
6
5
4
3
2
1

8 7 6 5 4 3 2 1

☐ Color 1

■ Color 2

▨ Color 3

☐ Color 4

▨ Color 5

⟍ Decrease left leaning

⟋ Decrease right leaning

Lautarferð
ÍSTEX Léttlopi
C1: 0086 Light Beige
C2: 0053 Acorn
C3: 9421 Celery Green
C4: 1419 Barley
C5: 0005 Black Heather

alantarfer8
ÍSTEX Léttlopi
C1: 0085 Oatmeal
C2: 9427 Rust
C3: 1404 Glacier Blue
C4: 0005 Black Heather
C5: 0051 White

Lautarferð
ÍSTEX Léttlopi +
BROOKLYN TWEED Tones
C1: Léttlopi 0056 Light Grey
C2: Tones Melba Overtone
C3: Léttlopi 0053 Acorn
C4: Léttlopi 1419 Barley
C5: Léttlopi 1702 Milkyway

Lautarferð
ÍSTEX Léttlopi
C1: 1703 Mimosa
C2: 1412 Pink
C3: 1404 Glacier Blue
C4: 1414 Violet
C5: 0051 White

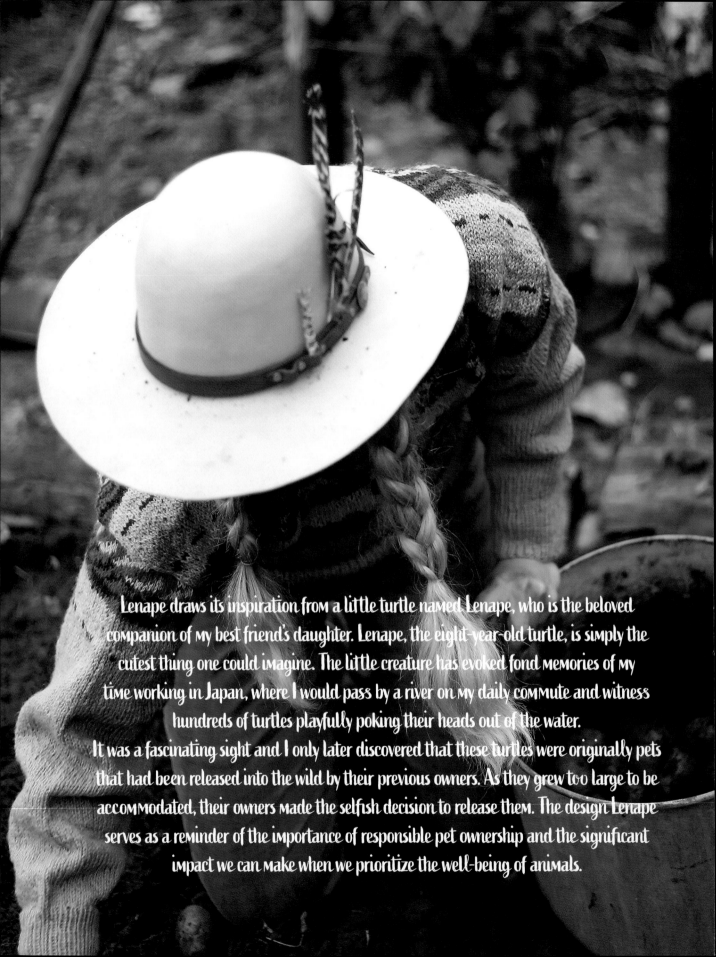

Lenape draws its inspiration from a little turtle named Lenape, who is the beloved companion of my best friend's daughter. Lenape, the eight-year-old turtle, is simply the cutest thing one could imagine. The little creature has evoked fond memories of my time working in Japan, where I would pass by a river on my daily commute and witness hundreds of turtles playfully poking their heads out of the water.

It was a fascinating sight and I only later discovered that these turtles were originally pets that had been released into the wild by their previous owners. As they grew too large to be accommodated, their owners made the selfish decision to release them. The design Lenape serves as a reminder of the importance of responsible pet ownership and the significant impact we can make when we prioritize the well-being of animals.

Lenape

Lenape

Starting with a ribbed hem, the body and sleeves are worked bottom up in the round and knit separately. A steek is added to the body for later sleeve attachment. The neck is knitted by picking up stitches from the body. The sleeves are knitted separately and sewn into the body afterwards.

Sizes
(2XS, XS, S) (M, L, XL) (2XL, 3XL, 4XL)

Recommended ease: 2–4 in (5–10 cm) positive ease

Measurements
Chest circumference:
(28.8, 32, 35.5) (38.5, 41.7, 45.4) (48.2, 51.3, 55) in/
(73, 81, 90) (98, 106, 115) (122, 130, 140) cm

Arm circumference:
(13.4, 13.4, 16.2) (16.2, 16.2, 18.6) (18.6, 20.9, 20.9) in/
(34, 34, 41) (41, 41, 47) (47, 53, 53) cm

Yarn
Kelbourne Woolens Andorra; sport weight; 60% Merino wool/20% Highland wool; 20% mohair; 185 yd (169 m), 1.8 oz (50 g) per skein

C1: 516 Lavender : (8, 8, 10) (10, 10, 10) (12, 14, 14) skeins
C2: 105 Snow White : (1, 1, 1) (2, 2, 2) (2, 3, 3) skeins
C3: 255 Camel: (1, 1, 1) (2, 2, 2) (2, 3, 3) skeins
C4: 001 Raven: (1, 1, 1) (2, 2, 2) (2, 3, 3) skeins
C5: 665 Salmon Pink: (1, 1, 1) (2, 2, 2) (2, 3, 3) skeins

Needles
Double-pointed needles: US 2 and US 4 (3 mm and 3.5 mm)
(unless the magic loop technique is used)
Circular needles, 16 in (40 cm): US 2 and US 4 (3 mm and 3.5 mm)
Circular needles, 32 in (80 cm): US 2 and US 4 (3 mm and 3.5 mm)

Gauge
22 stitches and 32 rows = 4 in (10 cm) on US 4 needle in stockinette stitch

Body

Cast on (162, 180, 198) (216, 234, 252) (270, 288, 306) stitches with C1 using size US 2 (3 mm) circular needle. Place a stitch marker to mark the start of the round and after (81, 90, 99) (108, 117, 126) (135, 144, 153) stitches to mark the front and back sides. Work "knit 1, purl 1" rib for 2.75 in (7 cm).
Change to size US 4 (3.5 mm) needle.
Continue in stockinette stitch until work measures (13.8, 14.2, 14.6) (14.6, 15, 15) (15.4, 15.4, 15.4) in/ (35, 36, 37) (37, 38, 38) (39, 39, 39) cm or desired length, allowing 11.4 in (29 cm) for Chart A.
Knit Chart for (2.6, 2.6, 1.7) (1.6, 1.4, 1.4) (1.2, 1.2, 0.8) in/(6, 6, 4.5) (4, 3.5, 3.5) (3, 3, 2) cm. From here you can choose between knitting the front piece and the back piece back and forth, or adding 3 extra stitches in between the front piece and the back piece on each side if you prefer to knit in the round and cut the armholes.
Continue Chart A until end.
Set middle (40, 42, 44) (48, 48, 52) (52, 55, 55) stitches from the front piece and the middle (40, 42, 44) (48, 48, 52) (52, 55, 55) stitches from the back piece on a size US 2 (3 mm) needle. You should now have (82, 86, 88) (94, 94, 106) (106, 112, 112) stitches. The remaining stitches form the shoulders and are sewn together or Kitchener grafted at the end. Work "knit 1, purl 1" rib for 1.2 in (3 cm).
Change to C1 and knit 1 round first and then purl 1 round.
Knit 1.2 in (3 cm) in stockinette stitch and loosely bind off. Fold inwards and sew in neck. Set the work aside and knit the sleeves.

Sleeves

Cast on (46, 46, 48) (48, 48, 52) (52, 52, 56) stitches with C1 using size US 2 (3 mm) circular needle. Place a stitch marker to mark the start of the round. Work "knit 1, purl 1" rib for 2.75 in (7 cm). Change to size US 4 (3.5 mm) needle. Continue in stockinette stitch increasing 2 stitches every 5th round (1 stitch after the first stitch of the round, and 1 stitch before the last st of the round) until you have (75, 75, 91) (91, 91, 104) (104, 117, 117) stitches. Continue in stockinette stitch until work measures (12.6, 12.6, 13.4) (13.4, 14.2, 14.2) (15, 15, 15) in/ (32, 32, 34) (34, 36, 36) (38, 38, 38) cm or desired length less 5.5 in (14 cm) for Chart B. Work pattern according to Chart B, letting increases run into pattern if remaining. Once the chart is finished bind off loosely.
Knit the second sleeve like the first.

Finishing

Sew or Kitchener graft shoulders together.

If you choose to knit in a round: Sew two tight seams by hand or with a sewing machine corresponding to the width at the top of the sleeves, and then cut up between the seams. Set in sleeves.

If you choose to knit back and forth: Set in sleeves.

Afterward, weave in all ends, block the garment, and lay it flat to dry.

Chart B

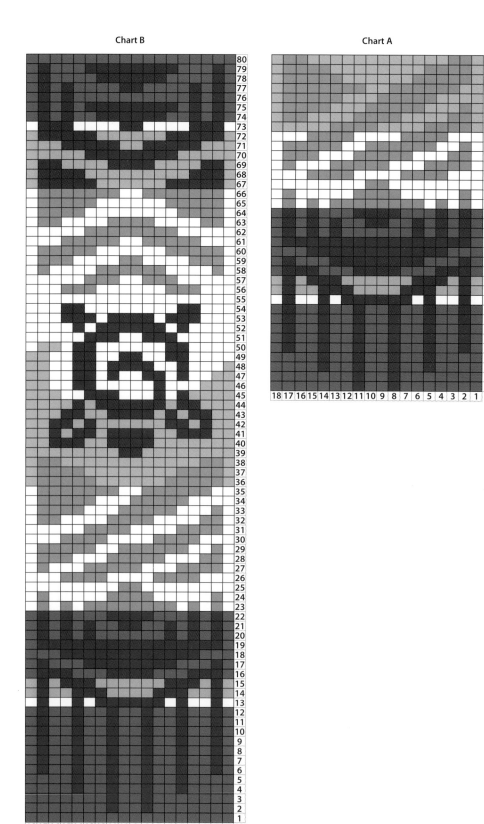

Chart A

■ Color 1
□ Color 2
▨ Color 3
■ Color 4
▨ Color 5

Knit Wild

Lenape
BERROCO Vintage DK
C1: 2105 Oats
C2: 2103 Mocha
C3: 21197 Cotton Candy
C4: 21193 Guava
C5: 2173 Red Pepper

Lenape
BERROCO Vintage DK
C1: 2153 Blue Note
C2: 2101 Mochi
C3: 2121 Sunny
C4: 2134 Sour Cherry
C5: 2177 Douglas Fir

Lenape
BERROCO Vintage DK
C1: 21191 Blue Moon
C2: 2101 Mochi
C3: 2121 Sunny
C4: 2145 Cast Iron
C5: 21193 Guava

Bearheart

The bear embodies noble qualities: strength, bravery, and courage.
These attributes hold immense significance in facing life's battles and conquering
the seemingly invincible. Life presents us with various challenges, and often it
requires a resilient "bear heart" to confront and overcome them.
Publishing a book is just one of them. This sweater is my personal favorite.

Bearheart

This pattern is seamlessly worked in the round from the bottom up. First, the body and sleeves are worked separately. Then, the body and sleeves are joined to form the yoke, which is shaped with decreases and worked in the round on a circular needle. The sweater is finished with a turtleneck.

Sizes
(2XS, XS, S) (M, L, XL) (2XL, 3XL, 4XL)

Measurements
Chest circumference:
(33.7, 36.0, 38.3) (40.5, 42.7, 45.0) (47.2, 49.5, 52.9) in/
(86, 91, 97) (103, 109, 114) (120, 126, 134) cm

Arm circumference:
(13.4, 14.6, 14.6) (15.8, 15.8, 16.9) (18.1, 19.3, 20.1) in/
(34, 37, 37) (40, 40, 43) (46, 49, 51) cm

Yarn
Istex Plötulopi (2 strands held together); pencil roving;
100% new Icelandic wool; 328.1 yd (300 m), 3.5 oz (100 g) per disk

C1: 1032 Chocolate: (3, 3, 4) (4, 5, 5) (6, 6, 7) disks
C2: 2020 Dark Woods: (1, 1, 1) (1, 1, 1) (1, 1, 1) disks
C3: 1030 Oatmeal: (1, 1, 1) (1, 1, 1) (1, 1, 1) disks
C4: 1027 Light Grey: (1, 1, 1) (1, 1, 1) (1, 1, 1) disks
C5: 1026 Ash: (1, 1, 1) (1, 1, 1) (1, 1, 1) disks
C6: 1038 Ivory Beige: (1, 1, 1) (1, 1, 1) (1, 1, 1) disks
C7: 0001 White: (1, 1, 1) (1, 1, 1) (1, 1, 1) disks

Needles
Double-pointed needles: US 7 and US 10 (4.5 mm and 6 mm)
(unless the magic loop technique is used)
Circular needles, 16 in (40 cm): US 7 and US 10 (4.5 mm and 6 mm)
Circular needles, 32 in (80 cm): US 7 and US 10 (4.5 mm and 6 mm)

Gauge
14 stitches and 20 rows = 4 in (10 cm) on size US 10
needle in stockinette stitch
Note: If working with Istex Plötulopi or similar weight yarn, hold two strands of yarn together throughout this pattern. Be sure to check gauge.

Body

Cast on (120, 128, 136) (144, 152, 160) (168, 176, 188) stitches with C1 using size US 7 (4.5 mm) circular needle. Place a stitch marker to mark the beginning of the round and after (60, 64, 68) (72, 76, 80) (84, 88, 94) stitches to mark the front and back pieces.

Work "knit 1, purl 1" rib for 3 in (7.5 cm).

Change to a US 10 (6 mm) circular needle. Continue in stockinette stitch with C1 until piece measures (12.6, 12.6, 12.6) (13.4, 14.2, 15.0) (15.0, 15.0, 15.7) in/(32, 32, 32) (34, 36, 38) (38, 38, 40) cm or desired length, allowing 3.5 in (9 cm) for Chart A.

Work pattern according to Chart A.

Place (6, 6, 6) (6, 6, 6) (7, 6, 6) stitches of the beginning of the round and the last (6, 6, 6) (6, 6, 6) (7, 6, 5) stitches onto a stitch holder or waste yarn for underarm, a total of (12, 12, 12) (12, 12, 12) (14, 12, 11) stitches. The stitches for the other armhole will be placed on holder when you start the yoke. Set the work aside and knit sleeves.

Sleeves

Cast on (32, 32, 34) (34, 36, 38) (40, 42, 44) stitches with C1 using size US 7 (4.5 mm) circular needle. Place a stitch marker to mark the beginning of the round.

Work "knit 1, purl 1" rib for 3 in (7.5 cm).

Change to a US 10 (6 mm) circular needle. Continue in stockinette stitch increasing 2 stitches every 5th round (1 stitch after the first stitch of the round, and 1 stitch before the last st of the round) until you have (48, 52, 52) (56, 56, 60) (64, 68, 72) stitches.

Continue in stockinette stitch until work measures (14.2, 14.2, 14.6) (15.0, 15.4, 15.7) (15.7, 16.1, 16.1) in/ (36, 36, 37) (38, 39, 40) (40, 41, 41) cm or desired length, allowing 3.5 in (9 cm) for Chart A.

Work pattern according to Chart A.

Place (6, 6, 6) (6, 6, 6) (7, 6, 6) stitches of the beginning of the round and the last (6, 6, 7) (6, 6, 6) (7, 6, 5) stitches onto a stitch holder or waste yarn for underarm, a total of (12, 12, 13) (12, 12, 11) (14, 12, 11) stitches.

Knit the second sleeve like the first.

Yoke

Join the body and sleeves on size US 10 (6 mm) circular needle. Place a stitch marker to mark the beginning of the round at the first join. Work stockinette stitch over the first sleeve. Then knit the front piece of the body and place the next (12, 12, 13) (12, 12, 11) (14, 12, 11) stitches on a stitch holder for the armholes. Knit over the other sleeve and back piece. You should now have (168, 182, 192) (208, 216, 234) (240, 264, 288) stitches.

Work the pattern according to Chart B and decrease as directed. Change to a shorter needle when needed.

Neck

Change to size US 7 (4.5 mm) needle. Knit 1 round and decrease to (68, 68, 72) (72, 80, 84) (84, 88, 92) stitches.

Work "knit 2, purl 2" rib for 8 in (20 cm). Bind off loosely.

Finishing

Graft underarm stitches to close. Weave in all ends. Block and lay flat to dry. Fold the neck

Chart B for sizes : (2XS, S, L) (2XL, 3XL, 4XL)

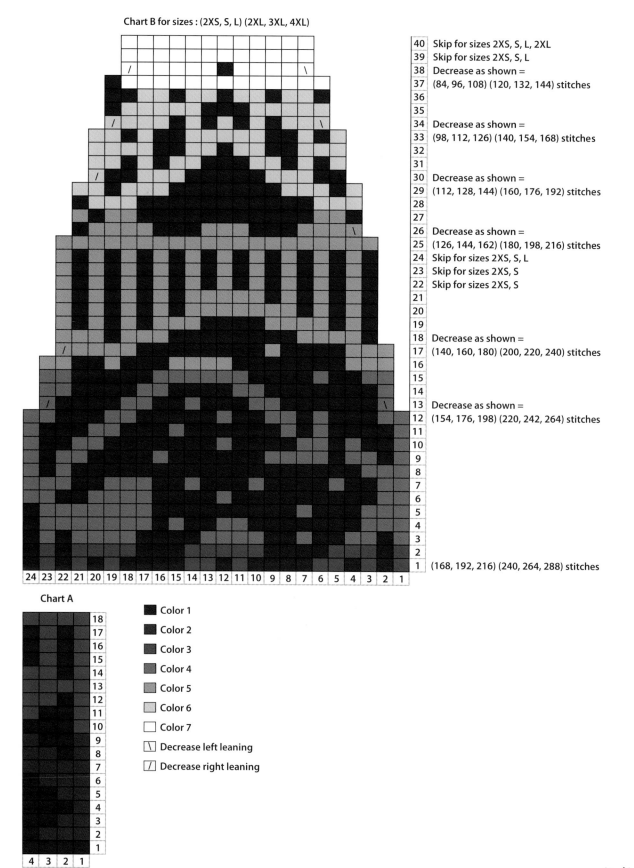

Row	Instruction
40	Skip for sizes 2XS, S, L, 2XL
39	Skip for sizes 2XS, S, L
38	Decrease as shown =
37	(84, 96, 108) (120, 132, 144) stitches
36	
35	
34	Decrease as shown =
33	(98, 112, 126) (140, 154, 168) stitches
32	
31	
30	Decrease as shown =
29	(112, 128, 144) (160, 176, 192) stitches
28	
27	
26	Decrease as shown =
25	(126, 144, 162) (180, 198, 216) stitches
24	Skip for sizes 2XS, S, L
23	Skip for sizes 2XS, S
22	Skip for sizes 2XS, S
21	
20	
19	
18	Decrease as shown =
17	(140, 160, 180) (200, 220, 240) stitches
16	
15	
14	
13	Decrease as shown =
12	(154, 176, 198) (220, 242, 264) stitches
11	
10	
9	
8	
7	
6	
5	
4	
3	
2	
1	(168, 192, 216) (240, 264, 288) stitches

Column numbers: 24 23 22 21 20 19 18 17 16 15 14 13 12 11 10 9 8 7 6 5 4 3 2 1

Chart A

Row numbers: 18 17 16 15 14 13 12 11 10 9 8 7 6 5 4 3 2 1

Column numbers: 4 3 2 1

Legend:

- ■ Color 1
- ■ Color 2
- ■ Color 3
- ■ Color 4
- ■ Color 5
- ■ Color 6
- □ Color 7
- \ Decrease left leaning
- / Decrease right leaning

Knit Wild

Chart B for sizes : (XS, M, XL)

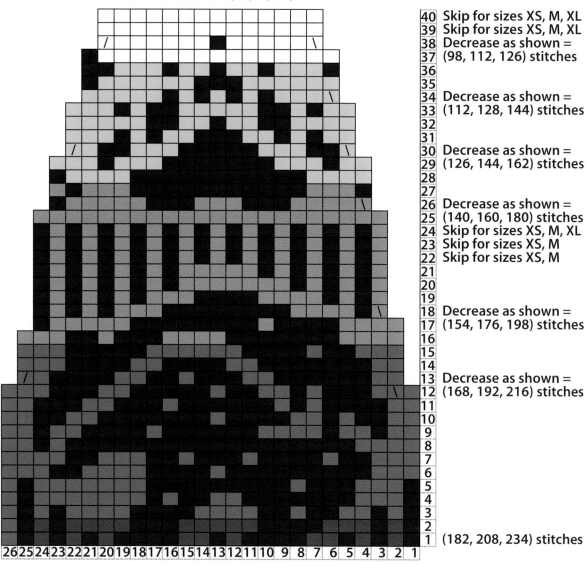

40 Skip for sizes XS, M, XL
39 Skip for sizes XS, M, XL
38 Decrease as shown =
37 (98, 112, 126) stitches
36
35
34 Decrease as shown =
33 (112, 128, 144) stitches
32
31
30 Decrease as shown =
29 (126, 144, 162) stitches
28
27
26 Decrease as shown =
25 (140, 160, 180) stitches
24 Skip for sizes XS, M, XL
23 Skip for sizes XS, M
22 Skip for sizes XS, M
21
20
19
18 Decrease as shown =
17 (154, 176, 198) stitches
16
15
14
13 Decrease as shown =
12 (168, 192, 216) stitches
11
10
9
8
7
6
5
4
3
2
1 (182, 208, 234) stitches

26 25 24 23 22 21 20 19 18 17 16 15 14 13 12 11 10 9 8 7 6 5 4 3 2 1

- ■ Color 1
- ■ Color 2
- ■ Color 3
- ■ Color 4
- ■ Color 5
- □ Color 6
- □ Color 7
- ⟍ Decrease left leaning
- ⟋ Decrease right leaning

Knit Wild

Bearheart
ÍSTEX Plötulopi
C1: 2027 Wine Red
C2(C3): 1430 Carmine Red
C4: 1426 Dark Amber
C5: 2028 Golden Blush
C6(C7): 1424 Golden Yellow

Bearheart
LION BRAND YARN Fishermen's
Wool held double + KNIT PICKS
Wool of the Andes Worsted held
double
C1: Fishermen's Wool Oatmeal
C2 (C5, C7): Wool of the Andes
Worsted Chestnut
C4: Wool of the Andes Worsted
Larch Heather
C6: Wool of the Andes Worsted
Garnet Heather

Bearheart
ÍSTEX Álafosslopi + EINRUM L
C1: 9103 Dark Grey
C2-C7: 0005 Black Heather
Details: Einrum L-Yarn 2016 Suspis

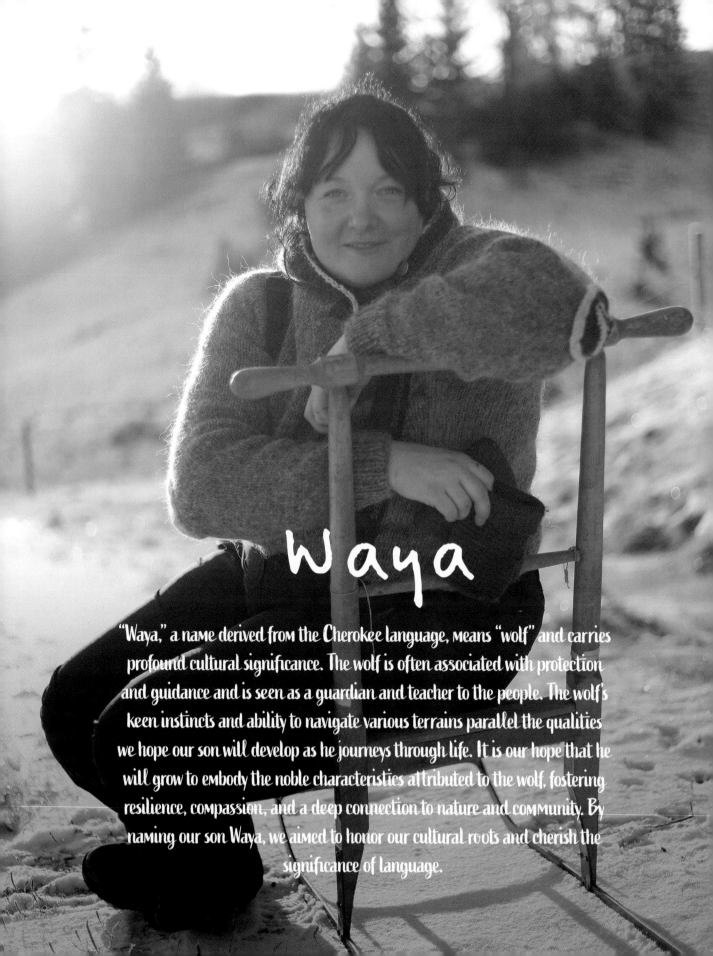

Waya

"Waya," a name derived from the Cherokee language, means "wolf" and carries profound cultural significance. The wolf is often associated with protection and guidance and is seen as a guardian and teacher to the people. The wolf's keen instincts and ability to navigate various terrains parallel the qualities we hope our son will develop as he journeys through life. It is our hope that he will grow to embody the noble characteristics attributed to the wolf, fostering resilience, compassion, and a deep connection to nature and community. By naming our son Waya, we aimed to honor our cultural roots and cherish the significance of language.

Waya

This pattern is worked seamlessly in the round from the bottom up. First, the body and sleeves are worked separately. Then, the body and sleeves are joined to form the yoke, which is worked in the round on a circular needle and shaped with decreases to achieve a raglan fit. Waya can be knitted with a turtleneck or a hood. Elbow patches are added at the end. Waya is meant to fit very oversized for that favorite sweater comfort feeling.

Sizes
(2XS, XS, S) (M, L, XL) (2XL, 3XL, 4XL)

Recommended ease: 4–8 in (10–20 cm) positive ease

Measurements
Chest circumference:
(36, 39.75, 43) (46.5, 49.5, 53) (56.5, 59.5, 63) in/
(92, 101, 109) (118, 126, 136) (143, 151, 160) cm

Arm circumference:
(13.25, 14, 15) (15.75, 16.5, 17.25) (18, 18.75, 19.5) in/
(34, 36, 38) (40, 42, 44) (46, 48, 50) cm

Yarn
Ístex Léttlopi; worsted weight; 100% new Icelandic wool;
109 yd (99.5 m), 1.8 oz (50 g) per skein

C1: 0057 Grey: (6, 7, 8) (9, 10, 11) (12, 13, 14) skeins
C2: 1409 Garnet Red: (1, 1, 1) (1, 1, 1) (1, 1, 1) skein
C3: 0054 Ash: (1, 1, 1) (1, 1, 1) (1, 1, 1) skein

Needles
Double-pointed needles: US 4 and US 6 (3.5 mm and 4 mm) (unless the magic loop technique is used)
Circular needles, 16 in (40 cm): US 4 and US 6 (3.5 mm and 4 mm)
Circular needles, 32 in (80 cm): US 4 and US 6 (3.5 mm and 4 mm)

Gauge
19 stitches and 28 rows = 4 in (10 cm) on US 6 needle in stockinette stitch

Body

Cast on (176, 192, 208) (224, 240, 256) (272, 288, 304) stitches with C1 using size US 4 (3.5 mm) circular needle. Place a stitch marker at the beginning of the round and a second stitch marker after (88, 96, 104) (112, 120, 128) (136, 144, 152) stitches to mark the front and back sides.

Work "knit 1, purl 1" rib for 2.75 in (7 cm). Change to US 6 (4 mm) size needle. Continue in stockinette stitch until work measures (16.5, 16.5, 16.5) (17.3, 18.1, 18.9) (18.9, 18.9, 19.7) in/(42, 42, 42) (44, 46, 48) (48, 48, 50) cm or desired length. Place (4, 5, 6) (7, 8, 9) (10, 11, 12) stitches at the beginning of the round and the last (4, 5, 6) (7, 8, 9) (10, 11, 12) stitches onto a stitch holder or waste yarn for underarm, a total of (8, 10, 12) (14, 16, 18) (20, 22, 24) stitches. The stitches for the other armhole will be placed on holder when you start the yoke. Set the work aside and knit sleeves.

Sleeves

Cast on (32, 34, 34) (36, 36, 38) (38, 40, 40) stitches with C1 using size US 4 (3.5 mm) needle. Place a stitch marker to mark the beginning of the round. Work "knit 1, purl 1" rib for 2.75 in (7 cm). Change to US 6 (4 mm) size needle. Continue in stockinette stitch increasing 2 stitches every 5th round (1 stitch after the first stitch of the round, and 1 stitch before the last st of the round) until you have (64, 68, 72) (76, 80, 84) (88, 92, 96) stitches. Continue in stockinette stitch until work measures (18.1, 18.1, 18.5) (18.9, 19.3, 19.7) (19.7, 20.1, 20.1) in/(46, 46, 47) (48, 49, 50) (50, 51, 51) cm or desired length. Place (4, 5, 6) (7, 8, 9) (10, 11, 12) stitches at the beginning of the round and the last (4, 5, 6) (7, 8, 9) (10, 11, 12) stitches onto a st holder or waste yarn for underarm, a total of (8, 10, 12) (14, 16, 18) (20, 22, 24) stitches. Knit the second sleeve like the first.

Yoke

Join the body and sleeves on a size US 6 (4 mm) circular needle. Place a stitch marker between every joining piece. Also, place an additional stitch marker at the first join to mark the start of the round = total of 4 markers placed (+1). Knit over the first sleeve, then knit the front piece. Place (8, 10, 12) (14, 16, 18) (20, 22, 24) stitches onto a stitch holder or waste yarn for underarm. Next, knit over the other sleeve and back piece. You should now have (272, 288, 304) (320, 336, 352) (368, 384, 400) stitches.

From here, we will shape the raglan.

Raglan Decrease: On each side of the marked stitches, decrease 1 stitch to the left and 1 stitch to the right (2 stitches per join), a total of 8 stitches decreased per round every 2nd round. On the right side of marker, decrease by knitting 2 stitches together through the back loops of the stitches. On the left side of the marker, decrease by knitting 2 stitches together. Change to a shorter circular needle if necessary.

Repeat decrease every other round until you have knit (6.25, 6.75, 7) (7.5, 7.75, 8.25) (8.75, 9, 9.5) in/ (16, 17, 18) (19, 20, 21) (22, 23, 24) cm from joining edge.

Decide if you want to knit a turtleneck or hood and follow the appropriate instructions below.

Turtleneck

Repeat decrease every other round for 2.25 in (6 cm) or until (72, 80, 80) (88, 88, 96) (96, 104, 104) stitches remain on needles.
Knit 1 round and decrease to (72, 80, 80) (84, 84, 88) (92, 96, 100) stitches.
Work "knit 2, purl 2" rib for 8 in (20 cm). Bind off loosely.

Hood

Bind off 7 stitches in the middle of the front of the sweater. This will be the new beginning of the round. From here on, the yoke is knit back and forth.

Repeat the decrease every other round and knit 2.25 in (6 cm) or until (72, 80, 80) (88, 88, 96) (96, 104, 104) stitches remain on the needles.

Knit 1 round and decrease to (72, 80, 80) (84, 84, 88) (92, 96, 100) stitches.

Place 1 stitch marker in the middle of the back. Knit back and forth in stockinette stitch until the hood measures 18.8 in (35 cm) or the desired length.

In the next 12 rounds, we will shape the top back side of the hood. The decreases take place on the left and right sides of the stitch marker placed at the back of the head. Decrease 1 stitch on each side of the marker every 2nd round, a total of 6 times (12 stitches decreased).

Graft the underarm stitches and the hood to close.

Hood Button Band

Pick up stitches for the button band as follows: Pick up 3 stitches, skip the 4th stitch, and repeat this pattern until you reach the other end of the hood. Make sure to end up with an even number of stitches.

Knit 1 row in stockinette stitch, then work the ribbing "knit 1, purl 1"

Repeat these rows until the button band measures 1.5 in (4 cm) on all sizes. If desired, knit buttonholes* on the left side of the hood; otherwise, skip this step for a hood without buttons.

Bind off in contrasting color and sew the bottom of the button band by laying the ends over each other. Hide the steeked edges.

*Buttonholes: After 0.8 in (2 cm), knit 2 stitches together and then bind off 1 stitch. Binding off 1 stitch will fit well with 0.8–0.86 in (20–22 mm) buttons. Continue until button band measures 1.5 in (4 cm) on all sizes. Bind off more stitches if you want larger buttons. Set the work aside and begin sleeves.

For a more detailed description in how to knit a button band see page 58.

Elbow Patches

Cast on 11 stitches using C2 on size US 6 (4 mm) needles. Do not join in a round but knit back and forth.

Follow the Chart and increase and decrease accordingly. Bind off loosely. Using C3 add an I-cord edging for a cleaner look.

Attach the patch on the elbow of the sweater.

Knit 2 patches in total, one for each side.

Finishing

Weave in all ends. Finally, block the garment and lay it flat to dry.

Chart Armpatch

Knit Wild

The Ketchikan Sweater

The picturesque town of Ketchikan, Alaska, feels like a second home to me. When I reflect on what makes Ketchikan an exceptional place, it's the lush forests and majestic mountains, the pristine waters and winding fjords, the variety of wildflowers that bloom in summer, and the captivating interplay of sun and moonlight on the mountains, casting its reflection upon the fjords during winter. Above all, I am drawn to the year-round spectacle of humpback whales gracefully encircling the shores.

The Ketchikan Sweater

This pattern is worked seamlessly in the round from the bottom up. First, the body and sleeves are worked up separately. Then, the body and sleeves are joined to form the yoke, which is worked in the round on a circular needle and shaped with decreases. The sweater is finished with an I-cord neckline.

Sizes
(2XS, XS, S) (M, L, XL) (2XL, 3XL, 4XL)

Recommended ease: 2 in (5 cm) positive ease

Measurements
Chest circumference:
(28.4, 31.9, 35.4) (39, 42.5, 46) (49.6, 53.1, 56.7) in/
(72, 81, 90) (99, 108, 117) (126, 135, 144) cm

Arm circumference:
(10.6, 11.8, 13.0) (14.2, 15.4, 16.5) (17.7, 18.9, 20.1) in/
(27, 30, 33) (36, 39, 42) (45, 48, 51) cm

Yarn
Kelbourne Woolens Scout; sport weight; 100% Corriedale and Merino wool;
185 yd (169 m), 1.8 oz (50 g) per skein

C1: 305 Moss Heather: (4, 4, 5) (5, 5, 6) (6, 7, 7) skeins
C2: 309 Juniper Heather: (1, 1, 1) (1, 1, 1) (1, 1, 1)) skeins
C3: 330 Meadow Heather: (1, 1, 1) (1, 1, 1) (1, 1, 1) skeins
C4: 703 Autumn Heather: (1, 1, 1) (1, 1, 1) (1, 1, 1) skeins
C5: 412 Navy Heather: (1, 1, 1) (1, 1, 1) (1, 1, 1) skeins
C6: 432 Teal Heather: (1, 1, 1) (1, 1, 1) (1, 1, 1) skeins
C7: 425 Blue Heather: (1, 1, 1) (1, 1, 1) (1, 1, 1) skeins
C8: 419 Ocean Heather: (1, 1, 1) (1, 1, 1) (1, 1, 1) skeins
C9: 709 Sunflower Heather: (1, 1, 1) (1, 1, 1) (1, 1, 1) skeins
C10: 667 Coral Heather: (1, 1, 1) (1, 1, 1) (1, 1, 1) skeins
C11: 614 Scarlet Heather: (1, 1, 1) (1, 1, 1) (1, 1, 1) skeins
C12: 105 Natural: (1, 1, 1) (1, 1, 1) (1, 1, 1) skeins

Needles
Double-pointed needles: US 4 and US 5 (3.5 mm and 3.75 mm)
(unless the magic loop technique is used)
Circular needles, 16 in (40 cm): US 4 and US 5 (3.5 mm and 3.75 mm)
Circular needles, 32 in (80 cm): US 4 and US 5 (3.5 mm and 3.75 mm)

Gauge
20 stitches and 30 rows = 4 in (10 cm) on US 5 (3.75 mm) needle in stockinette stitch

Body

Cast on (144, 162, 180) (198, 216, 234) (252, 270, 288) stitches with C1 using size US 4 (3.5 mm) circular needle. Place a stitch marker to mark the beginning of the round and after (72, 81, 90) (99, 108, 117) (126, 135, 144) stitches to mark the front and back pieces.

Work "knit 1, purl 1" rib for 4 in (10 cm). Change to a US 5 (3.75 mm) circular needle. Continue in stockinette stitch until work measures (16.6, 16.6, 16.6) (17.4, 18.2, 19) (19, 19, 19.8) in/(42, 42, 42) (44, 46, 48) (48, 48, 50) cm or desired length, allowing 2 in (5 cm) for Chart A.

Work Chart A

Place the first (8, 10, 12) (14, 16, 18) (20, 22, 24) stitches of the round on a holder or waste yarn. The stitches for the other armhole will be put on holder when you start the yoke. Set the work aside and begin sleeves.

Sleeves

Cast on (36, 36, 36) (36, 42, 42) (42, 48, 48) stitches with C1 using size US 4 (3.5 mm) circular needle. Place a stitch marker to mark the beginning of the round.

Work "knit 1, purl 1" rib for 4 in (10 cm). Change to size US 5 (3.75 mm) circular needle. Continue in stockinette stitch increasing 2 stitches every 5th round (1 stitch after the first stitch of the round, and 1 stitch before the last st of the round) until you have (54, 60, 66) (72, 78, 84) (90, 96, 102) stitches. Continue in stockinette stitch until work measures (18.25, 18.25, 18.5) (18.75, 19.25, 19.75) (19.75, 20, 20) in/(46, 46, 47) (48, 49, 50) (50, 51, 51) cm or desired length, allowing 2 in (5 cm) for Chart A.

Work Chart A.

Place the first (8, 10, 12) (14, 16, 18) (20, 22, 24) stitches of the round on a stitch holder or waste yarn. Knit the second sleeve like the first.

Yoke

Join body and sleeves on a US 5 (3.75 mm) circular needle. Place a stitch marker to mark the beginning of the round at the first join. Knit over the first sleeve. Work the front piece. Transfer next (8, 10, 12) (14, 16, 18) (20, 22, 24) stitches onto a stitch holder or waste yarn for underarm. Knit over the other sleeve and back piece. You should now have (220, 242, 264) (286, 308, 330) (352, 374, 396) stitches.

Work pattern according to Chart B and decrease as directed. Change to shorter needle when necessary. After completing chart (98, 112, 126) (140, 154, 168) (182, 196, 210) stitches remain on needles. Knit 1 round with C5, decreasing (14, 24, 32) (44, 50, 60) (62, 66, 76) stitches evenly over the round. You should now have (84, 88, 94) (96, 104, 108) (120, 130, 134) stitches on needles.

Neck

Change to size US 4 (3.5 mm) needle. Use applied I-cord bind off for neckline:

Cast on 3 stitches using backward loop method. Knit 2 stitches, then pass the first stitch over the second.

Repeat this pattern: Slip 3 stitches to the left needle, knit 2, pass the first over the second.

Keep 3 stitches on the right needle.

Use another needle to pick up a stitch from 1 row to the left.

Graft the 3 stitches on each needle together using Kitchener stitch.

Finishing

Graft the underarm stitches to close, then weave in all ends. Block the garment and lay it flat to dry.

Chart A

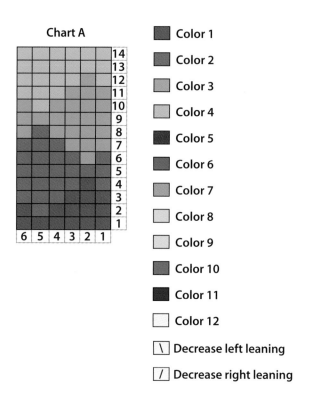

■	Color 1
■	Color 2
■	Color 3
■	Color 4
■	Color 5
■	Color 6
■	Color 7
■	Color 8
■	Color 9
■	Color 10
■	Color 11
□	Color 12
\	Decrease left leaning
/	Decrease right leaning

Chart B

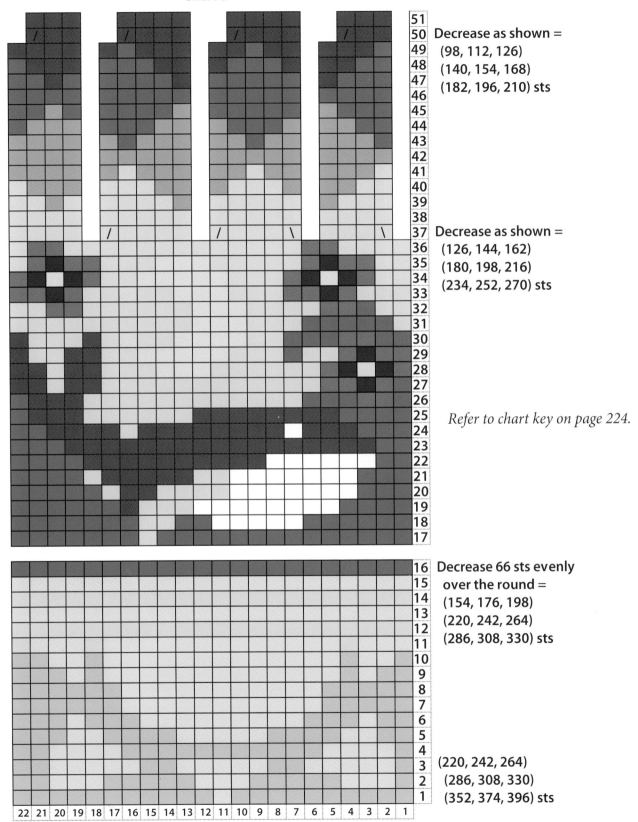

Decrease as shown =
(98, 112, 126)
(140, 154, 168)
(182, 196, 210) sts

Decrease as shown =
(126, 144, 162)
(180, 198, 216)
(234, 252, 270) sts

Refer to chart key on page 224.

Decrease 66 sts evenly
over the round =
(154, 176, 198)
(220, 242, 264)
(286, 308, 330) sts

(220, 242, 264)
(286, 308, 330)
(352, 374, 396) sts

The Ketchikan Sweater
KELBOURNE WOOLENS Scout
C1: 034 Graphite Heather
C2: 703 Autumn Heather
C3: 040 Pewter Heather
C4: 058 Gray Heather
C5: 026 Charcoal Heather
C6: 105 Natural
C7: 709 Sunflower Heather
C8: 690 Strawberry Heather

Thank You!

I want dedicate this book to my son,
the endless source of my happiness and my creativity.
A huge thank you to my family and friends, who provided technical and cultural
support and graciously fulfilled the role of my emotional rock.

Thank you for believing in me and pushing me to persevere when I was on the verge
of giving up, leading to the publication of my new book!

A special thanks goes out to my friend Trine-Lise and the talented photographers,
models, and knitters from around the world who played a vital role in bringing
Knit Wild to life. Your contributions and collaborations were
instrumental in creating this book.

I extend my deepest appreciation to the generous sponsors who provided the yarn
for the garments featured in this book: Brooklyn Tweed, Kelbourne Woolens,
Malabrigo, Istex, Spincycle, and Rauma. Your support made it possible to showcase
the beauty and diversity of these yarns in my designs.

I am immensely grateful to Stackpole Books for granting me the wonderful
opportunity to publish *Knit Wild*. Their support and encouragement have made
this dream come true, and I couldn't be more appreciative of their belief in my work.
I am truly honored to be able to share the beauty and creativity of *Knit Wild* with
knitters around the world.

To all the knitters who have enjoyed my patterns and helped make my dream of
becoming a knitting designer a reality: I am beyond grateful. Your enthusiasm and
joy in knitting my designs have given purpose to my work. I am incredibly proud
and filled with happiness knowing that I have had the opportunity to share my
creations with you. I eagerly anticipate the wonderful adventures that the garments
from the book will be a part of.

Thank you once again for your support and encouragement. Wishing you endless
joy and satisfaction on your knitting journey. Happy knitting!